Momma

for tillie, who said it was possible, & necessary; for mom; for lori & kia; for grandma & ritie; & reba; & shona & su & georgie & all mothers everywhere who love their children (& maybe even for those who dont). & for the men who are mothers, or anyway loving fathers. & for the children— o, its for all of us! me too!

Copyright © 1974 by Alta

Printed in U.S.A.
First Printing

Times Change Press
62 W. 14th St., NY NY 10011

Library of Congress Cataloging in Publication Data

Alta.
    Momma: a start on all the untold stories.

    Autobiographical.
    1.   Alta—Biography.   I.   Title.
PS3551.L76Z5   811'.5'4 [B]   74-79105
ISBN 0-87810-528-X
ISBN 0-87810-028-8 (pbk.)

Photographs by Reba Tokuhama

Momma

a start on all the untold stories

alta

TIMES CHANGE PRESS
62 W. 14th ST., NEW YORK, NY 10011

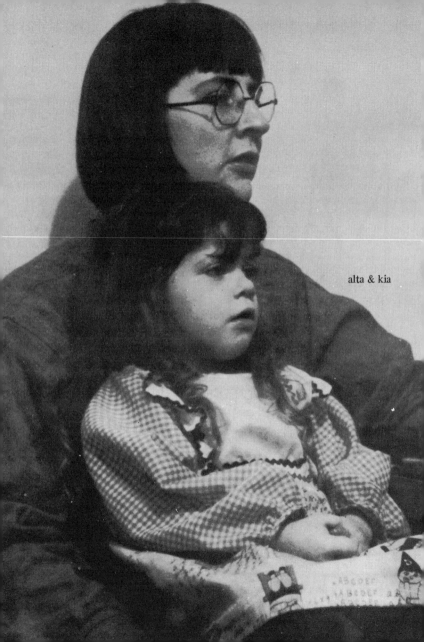

alta & kia

momma

1.

unbearable. unbearable to me. i would hear my own daughter's cries when i would get her from barbara's house—why did she cry every night when i came home? laugh and play all day, then see me & cry?

i took it as rejection.

i felt guilty.

yet it was her & me against the world. it wasnt the first time: we werent the only ones. her & me. i would go to school, get a degree, get a job (that was when i believed those were possible) & her father could drink his youth away. i had discovered i didnt need him.

2.

(o yeh? then why were you lonely? why did you go out with every man you could get yr hands on? why did you later live with simon?) i had discovered i didnt need him. wake up, rush lori thru breakfast, rush her to barbara's (i'll love her later, after school, its too hard in the morning, there just isnt enuf time), kiss her goodbye as i run out the door to catch the first of 3 busses to berkeley. to study literature at the university of california.

maybe it was because i told the teachers i could write, & i wasnt supposed to say that, *they* were; or maybe it was because they didnt like my writing. they nearly flunked me out of school. so much for plan 1.

"i need my mommy."

"*what* do you need! do you want a glass of water? what!"

how could i love her when no one loved me. how could i answer her need when no one wanted to hear of mine. and so i denied her.

i wanted to have another child because i love children & i miss having no baby. i was sorry the bleeding started. then why, when the doctor said "yr not pregnant" why did i reply "good" before i even

5

planned my reply. & the nurse standing right there: i was ashamed.

how could i possibly tell this story. it is too long. 8 years, every day of it, no one could even write one day. the minutes. history is so much simpler. but to say how she woke me at dawn with her little fingers patting my hand as i slept. "good morning mommy" & i wanted to always love like that: to love her & be loved like that: to love everyone, to pat everyone & never do an injury: we could all be so happy. would anyone believe it. in the united states, 1966. who could love. what fantasy.

or tucking her in when she was a baby. how she would smile & giggle in her sleep & i would bend over her blessed face, letting her laughter bless me. & her father lonely male in his chair with pipe & slippers & evening paper & not an honest feeling in his bones. she & i together. she & i against the world. always.

& the other mothers who had to fight for their children, & those who lost them: who the courts decreed are unfit to guide their children (that myth such a lie. as if we guided the children any more than they guide us. it was lori taught me how to love. no man, no adult. it was she who loved me more & more each day & who wanted to be loved more & more each day. if there was any marriage, it was not between me & her father.)

3.

& now the second girl. (before lori i wanted a boy. we were all supposed to. i was very obedient: i knew boys were exciting; you just let them grow & they entertained you. what could you possibly do with a girl? dress her in dresses? when she was born i was afraid: what does one do with a girl? now that the state does not drown them.)

the second girl. it took me a long time to feel comfortable with kia. she was over a year old before i did. the first year, she was her father's child: i had had her as a favor to him. he'd never shot his wad into a womb & produced a kid. i provided what you might call a service. so i let them love each other for a while. i was having none of it. & then i didnt understand her. she was not like lori at all.

getting used to a new child is like nothing else in the world. even getting used to a new husband is easier. you work with the first child, day after day, hours upon hours. in the night you rise with her cries.

6

then she grows beyond that & you adjust, each day, to the newness of the growing person in yr home. you think you learn her. & if a baby comes, you expect the same baby. a bit different looking, a bit different, but if the first did not cry you expect the second will not cry. at least i did. & almost felt like she was a different breed since she cried so much. "why are you crying?" i would cry back. "what more can i do? for gods sake!" but she would not stop. her cry, & my ears, & the house walls all around us. the older child playing by herself, or running out to play with friends. & kia & i trapped in the same cage: she unable to form the words that might get us out, & i desperately trying everything (babies dont cry in viet nam: everyone there loves the children, they all pick it up if it cries, & comfort it) but this isnt viet nam, & besides, babies cry there now because u.s. soldiers go there & torture them so they must cry now. the soldiers go to the one place its good & make it like here. why is she crying. & i am the mother.

men dont understand. some men, if they care for the child all day, come to understand the growing bit. the thrill of seeing thru children's eyes, the joy of being born. but how many men ever understand being the final mother? the one it all comes back to.

i pour honey into a jar & watch my life pour like sand pour out like sand, standing with honey o so slow as it oozes into the jar. why do i always stand & wait upon nature? is this how everyone lives? (is this how all women live.)

i be a poet and wonder how to feed the kids. i could sell out. i could live off a man again. i tried welfare & kept getting kicked off. i cannot bear that humiliation; that insecurity.

this morning i woke with a migraine headache. seeing a friend i love yesterday: i want my life to always be like that. to have no curtain between feeling & expression. leaving her i felt the curtain dropping down, surrounding me again: a city of people i love but do not feel free with. a city full of people afraid of me. cautious people. & i grow cautious: i lose myself to fear. so this morning the headache, the chores: dirty dishes, library books to return (overdue of course), a boxful of mail to answer: & the need to write, to say it all, to say my life is so full of sinks full of dishes, bills on the mantle; i wait until that so-called "work" is done, i wait to write. . . .

7

4.

but you know what i just did? i washed 6 cups & glasses & wanted to write down how i had to wash dishes & thot i cant stop until the other 13 dishes are washed & thot who says i cant stop & i thot well i just mustnt, thats all, & i thot bullshit i can too & i left the dishes in the sink & i sit here writing. but angel just sucked something up in the vacuum cleaner again & how dare i sit here writing instead of fixing the vacuum cleaner (wait! he's fixed it himself! no, its still clogged. a war. do i keep writing or get up & bang the tube until the tyrannical toy is loosened?) (how dare i say tyrannical toy? dont i love my children?) & i just asked what was in there & he doesnt know—i assumed it was a toy because it was near lori's desk—does that mean i'm a bad mother?

what is it like to be a mother in this country. what is it like to love yr children, to want to be good with them & to be too frantic to have the patience. what is it like to raise children with no help. 10 million mothers each alone, raising their children. its crazy, thats obvious, (& they lock us up if we cant handle it. we are maladjusted. no one would believe this if they didnt live under it) & for days we dont leave our cage. what is it like if, like some of us, you must work outside the home & then come home & work & love yr children & stories are clawing yr heart to get out but you have no time, no time. what is it like if, like me, you find yrself living a way you never expected, acting contrary to all yr self images, running around looking for yrself under every bushel & the words pour out all over dirty dishes, lapfuls of children, the man in yr arms, the woman in yr dreams, the words ever & always words words the blessed tyranny of words. who could say what it is like. it is easier to write about history.

my hands folded into themselves, i stare into my lap. so much to do. all those letters—

i must return to the dishes.

i'm back, the dishes not yet done. lightning hasnt struck yet. i used to have to finish one job before i could do another. the tyranny of duty. angel says he spends nearly all his time doing other than what he wants to do. i drew back in horror & said "but thats horrible! what if everybody lived like that!"

& he answered "most everybody does do it. thats why busses run

8

on schedule." (but i must do it too. all the times i've had a clean house. & no words on white sheets of paper.) we must allow ourselves to live. no one else is going to free us. stop ironing! stop it!

& i must call simon to remind him to take the kids to the eye doctor before our welfare gets cut off: 5 more days we can afford to be ill. then what.

i have postponed it as long as i can. i have washed the cups & glasses, organized my study, put folded cloth in my pants to soak up the blood, & there is no where to go now but this chair, this desk. i must face the agonizing hours, the days. (ah. a neighbor just came. she's gone now, but i am still geared to her. geared to speaking supersoft to counteract her nervous good humor.) am i finally learning how to be alone? its cool now outside but this house holds the heat. if i open the door for comfort, i will later spend half an hour killing the 20 flies that decide to visit. for every luxury i must pay either in time, energy or guilt. for the luxury of time alone i must feel guilty that i dont want loved ones with me all the time. & i must be lonely. heavy payments.

i set up my friend's picture on the desk (leaning against a kleenex box of unanswered letters) & i see her fixing food in her kitchen & waiting to be alone so she can work. my man has left already: hers does not go for 2 hours yet. everything looks so cluttered: i want to rip the newsclipping off the wall & clean up the floor. surely i can postpone the story of me & my daughters a few more hours.

5.

there is no beginning, thats one problem. it would maybe be easier if i could go chronologically: she was born, she grew; the next was born, is growing, the end. but last time we left the kids at simon's, lori ran along the sidewalk & she was tall, slender, like the twins before they moved to the philippines: she was that big. & i cried as angel & i drove away in the car. lori was 4 when simon & i moved into that house. the door fell off her room because i used to throw her on the bed & slam the door & finally it fell off & i stopped then. i cant remember if i stopped because the door finally did what i wanted & broke, or if by then i had met my lover & didnt need to slam the door anymore. lori was the one to pay for my frustration. & she had never hurt me. what i have done to my daughters.

this is unbearable. how can i write it. no wonder it is not written. or if it is written, not published. or if it is published, not recognized. no one could relate to such constant pain except another mother wishing to treat her children well. & how often are mothers also publishers?

that last paragraph was not nearly as painful as the one before. maybe i can avoid the real story until its told by innuendo. maybe i dont have to say how i have mistreated my children, how i love them, how i need them as much as i need privacy, how i have felt trapped for so many years, like nearly all mothers in this country, maybe all mothers all over the world, maybe all mothers forever, since the false history of the world began. maybe the story has not been told because the mothers living it had not the time. you must have time while yr in it, to tell the truth, maybe. i have seized that time.

gregory is walking to his house, crossing our lawn. hes all dusty & carrying a big rock. he comes to visit sometimes: he likes tea parties so i fix the tea while he sets up the little table & chairs, then we sit & sip our tea. he complains if there are no cookies. "my mommy always has cookies for our tea time" he says.

"good." i say. "lets have tea at yr house tomorrow." i am afraid to indulge his desire for lighted candles. visions of 4 year old kids with fire argh. but he gets candles at home too, candles & cookies & tea. his mother is an artist. but all she admits to are the drawings she does on the kid's lunch bags. i asked her if she had other drawings cause i'd like to see them if she did & she said "oh, no." later in our talk she admitted "sometimes i like to sit outside & sketch the houses & trees." theres a woman in every house. i think of that everytime i see hills full of houses. theres a woman in every one.

& the children so beautiful. they survive us, generally; they take our gift of life & live it. one day i was waiting for the light to change on shattuck avenue, lori in her stroller, & a woman came up to me & said "how could you. how could you have a child in this world. to bring it into this world." i understood so fully what she was saying, i made no reply.

"because i needed to." i would have said. "because i was lonely, without her." i would have said. which is just too selfish.

her & me against the world. (why does the world want to hurt us? why do so many people deliberately hurt us? & others are careless—how could her father go, & not see her for these 2 years? what is he made of, that he can ignore his own child. his soul must be dead.)

& when she was born, him saying "i wish i could say i love you. yr so beautiful, so strong. but i just cant say it if i dont feel it." & i saying "its ok. yr here, anyway." bullshit he was there. the walls were there too. they were of equal comfort.

6.

with simon it was different. but he said she looked like a stranger the first time he saw kia. & he felt so guilty about that that he knocked himself out being a good daddy for months after her birth. i missed the whole birth cause i was unconscious. that was different than the first one, too. by the time they let me see kia she had been outside for 12 hours. & it was 24 or more before i touched her. no wonder she cried so for the first few months. (does that follow?)

i sit staring at the lawn, my left hand on my belly. it is empty. bleeding. i make a home each month but there is no child to live in it. if i had not almost died with 3 of the other pregnancies, i would try again. i dont want to die. the only one that was physically easy was the 2 month miscarriage. but the depression lasted as long as a pregnancy would have / wombs are to suffer with.

thats crazy. i've said some boggled things in my life, but thats one of them. "wombs are to suffer with." they are also to house the children of yr body, of yr love. ideally. o fuck it. why do i have to decipher everything i say. sound like a damn english teacher.

the words pouring out of me like blood. but the birth difficult, & full of pain.

sometimes when the kids are here & i tuck them in & kiss them in their sleep, i think i would risk it all again & lie in bed for 9 months to have another child. but what if i died. i dont want to die. & what if my need for privacy is so strong & the help so minimal that i resented the child. better that i sit here, my hand on my empty bleeding womb. i can always borrow gregory. the children are not afraid of me. no child, except my first, my own. but she started fighting back when

11

she was 5, so she must not be too terrorized. it is only when we do not fight back that we are helplessly terrorized. like now i am not going to fight welfare. they are taking the money, the medi-cal, the food stamps. i dont know how we'll make it, but i cannot fight any more. i cannot crawl any more.

everyone tells us we cannot survive & we sit & stare & wonder if theyre right for awhile then we get back to work.

7.

i used to be proud of myself that i was the only mother i knew who had never severely beaten her child. i was The Better Mother. i only threw mine on the bed & slammed the door.

but no one writes of beating their child, you notice. we are all ashamed. we do not understand how we could so brutalize someone we love, even if we are brutalized ourselves. why must we carry on tradition? are we all english royalists?

i had grandma, who loved me & never beat me. not everyone has a grandma. my children, for instance. they have no grandma in the house to comfort them when i flee the house in rage, to walk until i can trust myself to hear their screams without striking out. they wait, frightened, until i return. i wonder if they are afraid i will not return. i am afraid of it, sometimes. when i run out i think "i cant take it! how can life be so horrible? how can i fight so with the kids?" & i walk & the neighborhood kids say "whereya goin?" not the ones i like; they dont ask. just the nosy snotnose kids ask. as if i knew.

i keep thinking of what i could write next & i keep thinking, o not that! that would take so long to go thru, so many pages of explanations; there must be an easier way. certainly a break for lunch is realistic.

well, team, i just had my lunch break. first i killed flies. (told you!) then i piddled around picking up papers off the floor. then i took out the garbage. then i called simon & reminded him to get the kids appointments with the doctors before the welfare runs out. then i called the dentist trying to find a dentist who will treat my broken tooth on medi-cal & couldnt find one. then i ate. then i ran out of excuses & here i am again.

writing often comes easy to me: it is my work; i love it. but *little* writing is what comes easy. big writing is scary. almost as scary as trying to draw. this is the first day that i have set up the back (bookroom) as my workshop since last spring. last spring people began to stay here so i moved my typewriter, etceteras out to the front room (where else would a woman write? how else could she watch the kids out the window while being immortal on paper? or how else could she hear the water boil? huh?) & the guests took over the back room. our last guest left a month ago. so i'm back. i've always loved sinks with windows over them so i can see out while i do the dishes. now you know what i got? a window over my desk. far out.

today i dont miss the kids so much. maybe its because i'm happy writing. maybe i can work & have children too. just like a man. remember that window i told you about thats over my desk? right. i want to quit writing & wash the window. what kind of house am i running, anyway? a dirty house? nobody will read my books if they kno i have a dirty house.

8.

i've been trying to remember if i loved lori's father. i used to try to remember while i was with him, too. it was hard, you can imagine, with him periodically telling me he didnt love me altho god knew i deserved it but he just couldnt. you can imagine i decided to pay him back & not love him either. (deserve? pay back?) unrequited love is not my strong point. (i just did another no no! the timer in the kitchen went off cause the eggs are done & i let it buzz til i wrote this paragraph! this is fun!)

there. i try to do one no no a day just to keep my hand in. but today is so full of no nos! i did bring back the windex from the kitchen since i had to go turn off the eggs. just so you wont think i'm neglectful.

i married him cause i wanted to be married, & he was the only man with sex appeal who was asking. it was a lovely proposal, too. he said "i have 17 dollars. you wanna get married?" how could i resist. besides, i thot i was pregnant.

i just got up & washed the window. i can just see an english professor trying to deal with that. "here the author uses the metaphor of washing windows to clear up his (sic) past, to see thru the future clearer with the added understanding of the past." (how come i flunked english? didnt that sound official?) well, it aint no metaphor, teach. i just got up & washed the fuckin window.

nobody even told me i had to. thats how fuckin dedicated a housewife i am, folks. i take care of my place.

did i love him. did he love me? we had a great honeymoon. the whole marriage was worth it because of the honeymoon, & the child. (conceived a year after our marriage. i was not, as it turned out, pregnant. i started bleeding walkin down the aisle. isnt that poetic. you can imagine me whispering to him "hey guess what. we didnt have to do this. theres blood running down my leg." & everybody throwing rice.

9.

i wanted to get married because it beat working for a living. & i later lived with simon because it, too, beat working for a living. besides, i got to preen while he read poems to me in public. i sat there looking modest & making sure everybody knew the poem was about me. nobody else in the room was looking modest. i was a groupie, was what i was. my first husband had told me i was too illiterate to be a writer, so i decided at least i could live with one & be a writer's mistress. i was determined to get glory somehow. did i love him either?

he used to show me his poems to other women. can you imagine? i hear there are other male poets who do that. if their wives suffer under that like i did, its a wonder theyre not all castrated by now. i must admit there were many nights i was tempted.

& so the second daughter. partly i had her as a favor to simon, partly as a companion for her sister. & maybe partly for me too altho after losing 2 i was just as ready to stop trying. i get discouraged by failure.

wow. the window even opens. what a fantastic workroom this is.

the thing i remember most about that pregnancy is how my "friends" disappeared. went away. did not call, did not visit. i lay in bed lonely & afraid, & i lay there alone with no adults to talk to except simon, for 200 out of 230 days. i can count still every visitor (an old boyfriend, a gay male poet, a gay woman poet, & a straight woman poet). i tried to make formulas, like, maybe poets dont desert you or maybe gay people dont desert you (my old boyfriend is bisexual) or maybe people who have lives of their own dont desert you (the ones who dropped out were all straight women, involved with men, & maybe they couldnt stand the added pain. thats what they said, anyway.) but whatever the formula, i learned not to count on the people who told me to count on them, & i tried desparately not to resent the child i was staying in bed to save. tried; & did not always succeed. but even in that prison, i was happy to feel her moving within me. i was happy to be able to not lose a 3rd child. we both nearly died. but we didnt die. & just 3 months after her birth i was able to break up with simon.

why?

i think because there were 3 of us finally. 3 of us against the world. lori & i no longer had to fight all by ourselves. & i understood that dinnertime would not be torture without a man there because there were enough of us to be happy company. no longer just a lonely mother & daughter. & so he went away.

he didnt want to go. he didnt understand how the hurt he had caused me could kill the love i felt for him. he kept saying he would stop screwing around; would help with the kids & the housework; would fuck me on my terms when i wanted to. but i was ecstatic with my new freedom. i took the kids with me to school where i taught, & we came home exhausted to eat peanut butter & celery & we laughed & i did not yell at the kids once. not for 4 months. can you imagine. i was that happy.

but the lover my body was so happy with didnt want me enuf to treat me right, so we broke up; & the school i taught at didnt want me enuf to pay for a babysitter for kia so i couldnt continue teaching & simon wanted to come back & i saw no alternative so he came back. it was better, cause he was trying, but i wanted more. i moved out after 7 months. kia stayed with him & lori went to her father. i had 3 weeks to figure out who i was, how i got where i was, & what to do.

stop. what can i say about that. so go on to the next phase: simon wanted the kids & so did i. he has them one week, i have them the next. its been like that for 2 years now. mostly it works.

(you cannot tell i stop to rest unless i tell you. this is too painful, &
i must stop.)

10.
why bother to tell all this anyway?

because i am sick of being alone! because i know every woman in
every house has her story & theyre not in books & we must begin to
tell how it is, to tell & share our lives with each other on intimate
levels.   thats why.

i dont want to get a job away from home. the children are here
only every other week, so i would see them only a quarter of the
time that way . . . this way we see each other half the time. its better.
but when theyre here, sometimes i get impatient. you can imagine
how guilty that makes me feel. why, if theyre gone so much, do i get
impatient the little time theyre here? i dont know. i wish i didnt. i'm
not on top of everything. maybe someday we'll be as happy again as
we were for those 4 months.

wow. i just stepped outside, picked a fig off the tree, & ate it. what
a life!

> mating robins
> fly into the fruit full fig tree.
> my headache is gone.

a cool breeze comes in the window.

i am a mother. i am a writer. will i ever be able to really believe
both those statements?

i'm humming mendlessohn's 5th song without words. his music is
gentle. no matter how hostile i am when i begin it, the hostility gets
lost as the music is released. i want this book to be like that. no
matter how hateful you feel now, i want to emotionally release you
into a feeling of warm human concern & joy. if you have felt my pain,
i want also to share my joy. the lamp, the cup of tea, the stillness. the
relief of feeling no physical pain.

it is so blessed to feel no pain. not even my knees hurt, & we
marched 10 miles across san francisco yesterday to protest the war. its
the farthest i've ever walked, without resting, in my life. & my knees
dont even hurt!

maybe life begins at 30? naw, life begins all the time. whenever its allowed to. life begins every time you have a child. if you need a reason for children to be precious, theres one. it is war & cruelty that slow the joy. i think we could all be happy. pass it on.

why is menstrual blood so shameful? its not like nobody does it.

11.

the kids next door came over to grown-up sit me. i went there after it got dark & said i'd heard noises in the patio. steve came over & gregory too. me & a teenager & a 4 year old gonna chase away a burglar. we got into the patio & gregory says "hey steve whydontcha pull out yr pocket knife?" we cant see anybody then the bushes move & we all freeze. steve says "i bet its a froggy." he lites a match, bends down & lo! a frog! we go out front where barbara is armed with her broom & steve says "it was just a froggy." i go back into the empty house, try to figure out which chair i'll feel secure in til angel gets home. a knock at the door. steve & lois (she also lives next door) with a deck of cards. they want to play 21 for money, but we dont have enuf for the rent this month & i'd feel like an ass losing my bus money. we play for free. angel gets home an hour later & the kids stand up: "well, bye. protect yrselves from frogs." lois read the first pages of this while she played cards. she wanted to see what i'd said about gregory. i asked her before she left what she thot & she said "i like it. i hope you make a lot of money."

12.

one nice thing about our kids having so many parents is that they get lots of grandparents. their grandad from new york (hes connected with the theatre) took them to the toy store today & bought them everything they wanted. the local grandparents are good for regular visits & holidays, & bunny & avivah are good for glamorous weekend swoops.

13.

lois treated us all at the donut shop & kia bit into hers & said "o! inside it is some bread!"

(see, there are happy parts. i'm sitting here trying to think of some others.)

14.

i've tried getting foster children. the first time was when lori & i lived with her father. a legitimate marriage, a house, a happy 2 year old; it sounded to us like a great place for another kid. so we got a social worker to psych us out. we had fingerprints taken, interviews, i took the minnesota multiphasic personality inventory to prove my sanity (i was in stockton state nuthouse for 3 months in 1962: suicide ward), we got letters of recommendation from doctors and neighbors. but we didnt get a kid. we would have taken any child; the so-called handicapped, the ones who were hard to place. but we got no children.

a year later the social worker came out again & asked if i would be willing to take 2 teenaged boys, recently orphaned. i said yes & asked why she had refused to take us the first time. she said " i never saw your baby cry." i looked at her, waiting for a more intelligible explanation. "your baby never cried! that was so unnatural i figured you gave her phenobarbitol to make a good impression. & if you were that desperate to make a good impression, what were your real motives?"

if you dont mistreat children, you cannot have one from the state. happy children do not exist, therefore yr child is an illusion. and so the state perpetuates itself.

we did get teenagers in our home: they came from juvenile hall & stayed til they were 18. there were 7 kids here over the space of a year & a half. for kids over 16 you dont need a license. i guess the theory being that they can defend themselves.

15.

when hope came to live with us, i lay down on the bunk bed i'd just bought so she'd have a place to sleep, & tried to realize her situation. what if i had been jailed, had been held prisoner. what if i had been held there because no one wanted me in their home. what if someone finally wanted a girl in their home: a girl from juvenile hall. why would they want me. why wouldnt anyone else want me. what if they didnt want *me* at all, but some kid they could save. a salvaged remnant. what if there were no charity, no acceptance. what if the room was cold. a new bed. a cold room. no one with whom to feel familiar. i lay there in bed & cried from loneliness. & i didnt want hope to feel lonely with us.

the car drove up. the state car, with the parole officer behind the wheel & a 15 year old girl in the front seat. i walked outside to greet her; she emerged from the car with a duffle bag & a stuffed animal. i was suddenly too shy to hug her or be coherent: what if she didnt like us. what if she didnt like me. as she walked toward me i realized her face was like mine: you knew just by looking at her that you could hurt her. & i didnt want her to be hurt anymore. we said hello shyly & the p.o. came in the house with us, to introduce us. i showed her the room: another foster kid in the other bed. a boy. which is why hope was only allowed to stay with us for one weekend. altho she was happy here & would have tried to make it on the outside, they took her away & put her in a home where the adults were rarely there, because our other foster child was a 16 year old boy.

she called me 2 weeks after being at the other house & said "i just thot i'd say goodby. let you know i'm going back."

"o, hope, no! how come?"

"i cant stand it out here. its horrible. i've got to go back. i'm gonna steal something but i wanted to call you first. just to let you know. too bad they wouldnt let me stay there: that might have been ok."

"bye, hope. i love you. take care."

"bye."

so she wrote a bad check in a drugstore & they arrested her for forgery & sent her back. they could have left her with me. the boy was no problem. she was a lesbian.

16.

after bo had moved out, the boy who had lived with us moved out, too. he was too upset that bo & i were breaking up: tim had done everything he could to get us together & it hadnt worked, & he loved us & wanted us together & when we broke up, tim got too depressed & moved out. so lori & i lived alone for a few weeks. one night when she was asleep & i was ready for bed, there was a knock on the door. i opened it cautiously & saw a tall, fuzzy headed kid. nobody i knew. he said "hal said i could come here." right off i was suspicious. hal acted irresponsibly in our home; we had arguments; i wasnt prepared

19

to welcome his friends. the kid stood there. he said "the cops are after me & i have no where else to go. can i come in?" i looked at him some more. what if i were a kid & the cops were after me? what if the one house i tried turned me down. but i'd never seen him & lori and i were alone. we are constantly being asked to sacrifice isaac.

so sure, i let him in, what the hell else could i do? & gave him a sleeping bag & went to bed. when i woke the next day, the dishes were washed, the floor swept, & he & lori were conversing pleasantly. she even had fresh milk in her bottle.

he kept promising that the world would be different when they grew up: acid, among other things, was going to show people the truth & the light. that was 5 years ago. this year, i heard where he was working & called & we were happy to talk & he promised to come see me the following wednesday & he phoned & said he had some errands, sorry; maybe some other time. i havent heard from him since. he grew up.

(retyping that, i wondered what lori said to him when she woke. i kno what kia would say "what you doin here? why you here?" what would lori have said. maybe "i dont kno who you are?" or "do you live here?") (rereading that, i see the chutzpah in saying i know what my 2nd daughter would say. maybe i dont, after all.)

17.

most kids, when theyre upset, threaten to run away. lori used to cry "i want to go home!"

kia told me tuesday, "if you dont stop yellin at me i'm gonna kick you outta this house!" (angel says shes never figured out shes littler than everybody else.)

18.

lori is like me when i was a kid plus the ways i wanted to be. i wanted to be a "tomboy" but was afraid to climb trees, afraid to roller skate, & the only boy i played with was allen, who was 2 years younger than i & did most anything i suggested. lori can do all that stuff; she can even walk up to a group of boys & ask to play with them. & she is as gentle as i was as a child: when a younger kid needs help on the playground, she goes to her immediately. at her peoples school (which she attends when she stays with simon), she started a little girls liberation. whenever a boy picks on one of the girls, all the other girls rush to her aid. ideally. sometimes, simon tells me, the girls just yell "lori!"

after i divorced her father & started living with simon, she told me one day i was to write a letter to her father: she would tell me what to say. she waited til i got a pen, then said,

" 'dear bo', cause you dont call him daddy, 'how am i supposed to open the windows without a husband. & how am i supposed to love you any more.' then sign yr name."

& last christmas she wrote in her notebook & then showed it to me "i know daddy has been an ass, but please forgive him. after all, it is christmas." i began to cry & she got worried & said she was writing about the man we live with now & then i got mad & said "well, he hasnt been an ass, why do you say that?" & cried & caused furor & she cried & later angel told me of course she was talking about her father, but she didnt want to hurt me so she said it was about him instead.

i think i must have been wrong to stress that relationship. if i could have just let him walk out of our lives & never mentioned him maybe she would have forgotten him. or adjusted completely to her 2 new fathers. or submerged her need. or some fool thing. last year when kids asked where her "real" father was she said "he died in the war." i wish he had.

but she remembers him & if she doesnt mention him for months, she does eventually anyway. she needs him. she wants to see him. & he has not even come into california for 2 years. so after a few scenes & a lot of yelling on my part, simon promised to drive her up to see her father. & her new sister & brother. & stepmother.

i ache when she is away.

19.

when i was bedridden with the second child in my belly, lori painted pictures in the morning until her teacher came to drive her to nursery school, came home & made peanut butter sandwiches for our lunch, played outside, brought her friends in to do plays & skits for me, answered the phone, told me stories & held my hand. when we thot i might be pregnant last month, she looked all worried & said "but thats too dangerous for you." i said yeh, but i miss not having a baby & she said "o mommy. well, if you are pregnant, i'll help you."

i rarely feel we have enuf time together. i cant just decide to be a good mother & hold her on my lap anymore; shes 8 years old! she wants to play outside, or do math, or watch t.v. but she sits with me for a few seconds as part of her keep mother pacified program. she gave me a surprise 30th birthday party & invited the kids next door plus barbara & 2 other women friends. cake & presents! i was sunning outside in the patio— i had to dash thru the kitchen where they were all laughing & put a dress on over my bikini. shes with simon this week. she & kia.

i called them on the phone yesterday & kia said "you come get me now."

"i cant, buns. i dont have a car."

"then you walk."

"its too far! its 20 miles!"

"you can walk it."

"well, youre coming back here in a few days, ok?"

"you walk over & come get me now."

"no, buns, i'll see you in a couple of days."

there was a pause while i felt guilty, then she asked, "you wanna talk to simon now?"

(if only i could have my children & my work too! this way i get ½ of each. its better than all of one, or none of either. but wouldnt it be wonderful to have the children & the work too? just like a man can—)

(but why can a man? because he is not total mother. because someone else usually takes top responsibility for the kids. if they skin their knee, his wife or babysitter or housekeeper washes it off while he does his work. even if i could afford it, i would never get a wife or hire a shitworker. its counterrevolutionary. but whats revolutionary? communes are no good for artists. & usually no good for mothers. what else is there?)

20.

i went from home to college to travel to apartment to marriage to nuthouse to marriage. so i had had nights where i didnt have to report in to anybody, but not, of course, since the kids were born. when john & i split, he watched the kids while i took off. as i walked away from the house, i thot, "this is the first night i have had to myself since 1962!" & i danced all the way to the corner.

21.

when angel read these first pages he became sad & i had to ask why. (he doesnt talk a lot.) he said "why arent you as happy as you were those 4 months?" & i answered immediately "because i was teaching." it was the only time, the only place i was allowed to teach. (may, 1973: susie & i just got kicked out of oakland hi cause i said playboy damaged people's ability to love, & held up a photo of myself in a kotex. the teacher kicked *us* out as obscene. & the boys lockers are still full of playmates.) anyhow. i had worked at the school for the blind in berkeley & enjoyed that, but that was just an hour a week. this was 3 hours, 2 days a week. the first semester, a humanities class & a poetry class; the second semester, women's history. i was asked to teach by the students themselves: florence came & said "hey, theres a school you can teach at! i'm going to be in it!" & i didnt believe her but she made me promise to go. i did. & i started teaching 4 days later.

i nursed kia during class. we listened to a tape of john oliver simon & i asked the kids to write poems about their impressions. it was fun, & after class, florence & i got ready to walk home. a tall, assertive kid said "eh! florence! tell that lady to put her bra back on!" some of the kids laughed.

i stepped into the room, stared at him, said "fuck you, kid" & walked out. i was scared & half expected a hand on my back as i carried kia down the stairs to her stroller. but there seemed to be no repercussions: for a couple of weeks timeo & i would glare at each other but that was about it.

a month or so later i touched his shoulder when he was lounging in the hall. he looked quietly at me. "shall we fight it out or shall we be friends?" i asked. he said "easier to be friends." we shook hands. at the staff meeting later that day, another teacher told me the kids had been saying timeo was mad & he & his knife were waiting to meet me alone. luckily i hadnt heard that earlier.

he & i circled each other, almost. we always knew where the other one was. but he came to a couple of classes & did well. naturally it turned out he was a fine artist.(i say naturally,because every time a kid has been described as difficult, demented, hostile or slow to learn, i find out they secretly write or make music or draw.)

i'm trying to write about timeo & me but i'm sitting in a pleasant coffee house listening to bob addison play guitar. its not the same atmosphere as that smelly school: this place is so hi class, how can i convey that school: the apartment house building with the smell of an auto shop next door. the dingy stairs inside, the rickity wood stairs outside. it was like climbing up to a subterranean dungeon. & everything reduced to essentials: we were all ages, colors, both sexes: we were all classes, from the main man with his 3 story hill house to me, the unwed welfare mother in the flatlands, to timeo in his faded 2 story house on 61st st, to rachel with her spacious home above the smog. at one meeting the kids were discussing trust & some of the rich white kids said they were shocked the school had to be locked up. rachel said she never locked up her house & t.k. said, quick as i write this, "whats yr address?"

i liked t.k. he would carry kia's stroller over the streets torn to make subways, & he would cuddle her when she fussed. (he later, as a joke, planned on hiding her from me in a trunk which i luckily discovered in time.) & he was tough. cops laid in wait for him. they liked to beat him until he passed out. & he was 14.

raquel was one of my heros. she loved t.k. & was as tough as he was. one day when i hurried eagerly up the stairs to class, i saw, instead of the usual kids slumped on the usual couch, i saw broken chairs, smashed lite bulbs, everything destroyed. the typewriter, the new musical instruments, everything. we stood there hurting & raquel bent to pick up some glass. it took all 70 students & 21 teachers working 3 hours to clean the school. as i was clearing out a corner, i heard mateo whisper to raquel "we shouldnt have done this." "shut up." she said. there was much speculation about who had done it & why. most kids thot outsiders, students from other schools. at a staff meeting, the teachers didnt even want to wonder who. the main man said "well, we're making progress." we all snorted. he continued: "thats right. they quit beating each other, you notice. its the building now. we're making progress."

the only loss i moaned was the instruments. only the drums were replaced.

but that, too, made me feel close to raquel. i feel undirected rage & i smash chairs. & i too repent afterward, & work hard to clean up.

22.

i was so blessed naive: lemme tell you this story. a school meeting. i'm at the bottom of the steps with kia. a couple of boys next to us. theyre being clever hostile, calling me a *lib er al la dy* who cries at oppression. i just listen. (24 hours later i came up with great replies.) filleppe says "mateo aint got no mommy. dont that just make you wanna cry?"

"yes, it does."

"o, you so soft hearted mama, you with yr jew husband."

"i dont have a husband."

"whered you get the kid?"

"outta my belly. i didnt marry her father."

"no shit."

so i'm sitting there relating to them, glad we're talking, & mateo sets the rug on fire.

i blow my cool. tears come to my eyes & i say "stop it."

"stop what, teach?"

i just look at him. he rubs the smoking wool with his shoe. main man leans over the balcony, sniffs. "whats happening."

"nothin, director. everythins cool."

main man looks at me. "its cool," i say. me & the kids. me & my daughters, me & raquel, me & filleppe & mateo. so main man asks again: "sure?"

"sure."

the meeting continues. its time for me to meet lori at her school. i say to the boys "time for me to go. see ya." i put kia in her stroller, wave goodbye & start off. filleppe calls me back. "hey teach. you forgot yr purse." i'm touched. i smile & thank him.

(do you get it, or are you as naive as i was? *the conversation was a front. they were ransacking my purse.* i didnt even catch on til a year later, when i heard how they steal from women's purses. thats how. they didnt steal from me, of course. somewhere in all that we did

make contact.)
so i walked on, basking in my new friendships, & met lori at her school.

23.
3 years ago simon & i were very political. thru his politics he heard of a new women's group. & he took me to the cafe to meet 2 of the women. they told me the time/date for the next meeting & simon drove me there & carried me up the stairs (i was pregnant by then & forbidden to walk). so for the last few weeks of my pregnancy, i was part of a weekly small group. except that it was large: there were 30 of us. we were all from previous politics. all of us were into, besides our women's group, at least one other political struggle. some of the women worked on the local underground paper, including the wife of that paper's editor. i called her one wednesday to remind her of the meeting & she said "o, alta, i'm sure youre the only one in the group still speaking to me." i asked why & when she explained the others were striking the paper & expected her to back their strike & were calling her a scab, i said "well, i'm sure youll be welcome tonite. do you want me to ask & then phone you again?" she did. so when the women arrived i explained how jane was foolishly worried that our outside political problems might bar her from being with us as a woman. i finished & waited smilingly for their response. well. it was my first experience with purging. cleansing of oneself by removing the filthy member. dangerous physically & no fun socially. when people's toes get infected, they dont cut them off. but maybe thats not a sensible analogy? anyhow, jane got infected by loving her husband more than 29 women she had known for 2 months, so she was uninvited. jeez did i feel stupid calling her back. "hey jane. you were right."

"yes, thats what i thot. well, thanks for trying."

but i stayed with the group. i always stay until i get purged. dont ask me why: maybe i'm just desperate for company. & we worked toward a city-wide conference for women. each women's group was to prepare papers on a topic. judy suggested "why dont you do a thing with poetry?" so it romped around in my head until one nite i decided to make up an anthology of all the poems i liked by women. i zoomed thru the bookshelves, pulled down all the women's books, & stared at them in horror. there were only 14. out of hundreds & hundreds of books. poetry, novels, astronomy, biology, geometry, history, psychology: of course there were books by women that i couldnt use for my poetry anthology, but how many of those left on the shelves were by women? jane austin. virginia wolff. & the rest? d.a. levy, jung, t.s. eliot, freud, shakespeare, malcolm x, emerson, richard krech, aristophanes, eldridge cleaver & 300 other men. either i had sold out my culture by denying its validity (& not buying the books) or i did not know of our culture & had been lied to all my life, or it did not exist. all the alternatives terrified me. in desperation i read all 14 poetry books & then pulled out the anthologies. i only found 6 poems relevant to the women's struggle.

for the next couple of weeks i begged friends to bring books from their homes, the library, 2nd hand stores. anything. i found one more poem. to those i added one of mine, one by magda that she had shown me at her house a few months earlier; i requested drawings by the artists on the block & out came the first *remember our fire*. simon printed 500 of them & people loved them. it was the first women's poetry collection any of us had ever seen. to celebrate, i planned a reading with the poets from that booklet. the reading was scheduled for 2 months after kia's birth.

five of the poets lived in the bay area. i called & 2 of them agreed gladly, i of course was eager, & i relate here the responses of the 2 others. julia said "what do you mean, a women's reading?" (told you we had never heard of such a thing.)
"i mean, just women. reading poetry. men can come listen if they want."
"just women. it'll be kind of flat, dont you think?"
but at least she came.
the 5th poet, the most famous for being revolutionary, said "o, yr from women's lib."
"yep."
"well, i dont go for all that. you all want to have abortions & work in factories."
"i'm having a baby in 2 weeks, & nobody wants to work in factories. where do you get this shit?"

"well, when's the reading." so i told her & asked if she would come, cause i didnt want to put her on the leaflet if she didnt. she said she would come, but she didnt like women's lib. in case i hadnt heard it the first time around.

so kia was born & she & i lay around sleeping & trying to adjust to a new world of separation, & a week after her birth my women's group gave me a shower: (we did not dare celebrate before, in case one or both of us died) there was champagne, a stroller, blankets, diapers, powder & lotion, & bubbly slim glasses of champagne! it was lovely, & i smiled & cried, totally surprised. & totally touched that this women's liberation group was not "beyond" celebrating the birth of a child.

i scheduled the reading for our meeting night, so everyone in the group could come. there were 50 or more people to hear us, but only 2 from my women's group. i thot there must be some mistake: all our meetings had at least 10 people. so we waited for them, & for the famous poet. but they never came & she never came.

we had our reading. when julia got to the mike, she said "i had no faith in this reading since it was to be all women. i thot it wouldnt be good. so i only brought 2 poems that i dont like very much, & now i'm ashamed." but the rest of us read poems we loved & the reading was a huge success. (youd think, since i'm a poet, i could say something less trite than "huge success"—but what? it was fun? people liked it? a lot? we all got revved up & wrote more poems? its all true—)

& at the next meeting of the women's group i cried out "you celebrated the birth of my daughter, & i was happy & touched. the other birth, the birth of my work as a woman poet, the birth of our culture made public, you had no faith in! you, too, see me as a vehicle for procreation! you, too, are afraid to believe in our culture!" everyone sat, ashamed, quiet, until judy said "its true."

& simon was mountain climbing that night. he didnt think the women's reading an important birth, either.

24.

i'm not only a mother; i'm a daughter. & like many of my generation, i judged mother heavily. i learned dutifully in school that a mother wore aprons, had curled blue-grey hair, & made peanut butter cookies with fork marks up & down & also sideways. thats how i would be when i grew up. i would be a good mother. whereas my mom was a bit weird.

she hates housework: reduces cooking to the essentials (vegetables in hot water on stove. meat in pan on hot stove.) & she knows the stock market & loves learning about real estate. the fact that she is a brilliant financier was lost on me until i found myself applying for welfare at the age of 29. i must have gone astray somewhere, to end up crawling in a barebones building with workers who know i am beneath them. scum of the earth, us welfare mothers. we do it on purpose.

so mom's financial speculations no longer seemed counter-revolutionary, they seemed like a survival mechanism that i could have respected all these years.

when i told her i was writing the story of a mother, she asked "how old are you making the mother?"
"well, its about me & the kids, so i'm 30 & the kids are 8 & 3."
"hm." she said.

so i started thinking: of course i cant write the older mother yet, except from the child's point of view. like my mom has been with me nearly 4 times as long as i've been with lori. shes seen me go thru a lot of idealogical changes, as well as the whole general growing up. like when i was 14 i tried to convert mom to jesus freakism. it wasnt christianity as most (civilized? ah, what words are etched in our intelligence!) people think of it: it was that sob yr sins out carry the cross around the world dont leave anybody alone jesusfreakism. the fact that my folks had always been religious in the extreme was conveniently bypassed: they werent jesus freaks, so they didnt know the meaning of Real Life. i dont know why i singled out mom: maybe because the thot of teaching her something was such a trip; maybe i thot christian science was the devil's invention; or maybe kathy told me to. kathy was the girl who introduced me to the joys of fighting sin. mom approved of her, of course: she was blond & sweet, always smiling, blond & sweet, smiling, blond, smiling & sweet. but she could afford it: all the while, she was waiting to snatch yr heart for the greater glory of jesus.

29

i dont know why she picked on me: maybe because i was always friendly to new kids in school, maybe because i looked like a guilty sinner. anyhow, i was the first from our 8th grade class to kneel at kathy's bed sobbing out my sins & praying, begging forgiveness from jesus who had done no-no's in his youth too & so understood. (that was my interpretation, anyway.) next to kneel was judy, & then we got sharon. we worked on carole & gwen all year but they had too much pride or something. (pride was a sin, of course.) so poor mom, being her usual loving self & hearing things like "i'm praying for you, mom. i dont want you to burn in hell." or whatever i said to her then. thinly disguised revenge, maybe; you spank me & i'll tell you you better pray or else go to hell? that lasted a year or so. my 8th grade yearbook is a source of embarrassment: all the kids signatures, instead of saying "good luck" say "to a wonderful chrisitan who helped me see light in darkness." & then theres the one that says (from the boy i had a crush on) "to the girl who showed me i have a good side." argh! dig the schizophrenia: good side / bad side. 2 inside of us, god & the devil. its a wonder we're not all off killing commies for the greater glory of the sinless. argh & double argh.

25.

people hate housewives. youve probly noticed. jokes about us: we couldnt have any brains or we wouldnt be doing this. & the women themselves (who the hell do i think i am? *our*selves–) say "o, i'm just a housewife." i remember a terrifying article in a woman's magazine: a woman whose husband was a famous shrink & author; she would think of her husband's vital work & see herself sitting home watching the kids watch t.v. & be in a blue funk for a week when her husband would finally notice & say whats wrong dear & she'd tell him & he'd again reassure her that her job was even more important than his (that why he didnt do it?) "because she was raising their sons who might also achieve glory if they had a devoted mother." so she wrote it all down & sent it to a mag & got paid for it & became a published writer.

why did a woman's mag print it? why, for instance, not *esquire*? undoubtedly she didnt send it there, but my point is that *esquire* never would print it. its not interesting from an action point of view (giving up one's life hardly qualifies as action). but even the men who do that to their wives would see her as stupid for going along with it. & nobody wants to read what stupid people do. being a wife is one of those games you lose even if you win.

people from cities constantly ask me how i can stand to live in the suburbs where there is no one but housewives. & everyone knows housewives watch *as the world turns* (yes, i do) & talk about recipes. well youd be amazed. every woman here has a life. someday there will be a massive jail break & youll get to meet her for yourself.

(ooh, & a couple of weeks ago (i'm retyping this ms.) a dream came true: angel & i had dinner with simon & jan his wife & angel liked the salad dressing simon had made & simon told him the recipe! whee!)

26.
kia's in the baby swing. shes the same age lori was when i used to push her in the swing every morning. there was nothing else to do, while waiting for the divorce. every morning after breakfast we would walk along the river to the park. there were ducks in the river: momma ducks with a train of babies behind them & i would hold lori's hand & when we got to the park, push her in the swing. i would try then, as i am trying now, to get away with 10 pushes & then rest. kia now is insisting "push me. push me. why you writin in that book?"
"more pushin!" she yells. i'm sitting at her side, the swing making shadows on this page. "more pushin, cause i'm stopped!"
"o, you are not stopped!"
"yes i are!"

after the park, lori & i would walk back to the boarding house & have lunch. then her nap. then we'd sit on the porch & watch the afternoon thunderstorms. dry on the porchswing, we'd watch the sky flash, & the heavy rain.

then dinner. then she'd stay with a girl in the boarding house while i went out with gangsters & got drunk.

in this park, as in the park in reno, there is another woman watching her children. a lot of men are on the other side of the fence, playing basketball. & the children swing & make houses with the sand.

& later, last nite, i turned off the t.v. when the girls were watching a horror show. lori screamed after me "i am not scared! cant you hear me! i am not scared!" & i retreated from her sobs to the kitchen where reba was waiting to say goodby after driving us home. her children moaning "i'm tired, mommy." she watched me while lori screamed from the other room; then kia rushed in, ran up to me & screamed "Aaaahhh!" in my face & ran back to her sister. reba & i tried to have a pleasant farewell, but could not & after she left i told the kids to get ready for bed. lori wouldnt do anything but cry about how i had turned off the t.v. & kia insisted on another type of toothpaste, which i refused her, & then she began again. off & on, calm moments where they would make attempts at getting in their pajamas, & hysterical accusations which i soon could no longer tolerate. i swatted the baby & walked out of the house, hoping to calm down outside. i could hear them screaming all the way out to the sidewalk. "mommy! mommy!" so i went back in. they didnt stop screaming & i started again myself so i went outside again. "mommy! i want my mommy!" again i went in. i tried to call angel; no answer. i called simon. he volunteered to talk to them. i gave the phone to lori & went outside again. 3 of the neighborhood cats climbed on my lap & i sat there getting bit by fleas & hearing "she turned off the t.v. . . ." & wondering how we could fight like this when i had been so miserable & lonely away from them all week. why dont things work out nice? what the hell do we have to do to get happy? & after the phone call i went in, again tried to hold kia, again couldnt stand the screaming, walked in the bedroom & picked up the pills, admonished myself "stop being dramatic. think what a trauma for you to kill yrself while everyone is still awake" & settled for 2 meprobamate 400's & tossed myself on the bed, face down. a few minutes later i heard the kids greet angel. then they came in to find me & ask how i was.

what an effort to write all this. lori cried for ages: one of the things she told us was that she always has to choose whether to get angry & risk our anger & possible injury, or hold hers in so that we wont get mad too. & talkin about injury, kia started the scream scene tonite again & i spanked her but she was lying on the rug & i hit my hand on the floor & swoll my middle finger all up. it stopped kia from crying, at least, but you oughtta see me tryin to type with a splint on.

the final scene with kia last nite was her climbing on me & asking "whats the matter mommy" & me muttering "i'm sad."
"why you sad?"
"cause of our fight."
"you sad cause of our fight?"
"uh-huh."

"o, poor altie." & she kissed me. she snuggled into my arms & fell asleep, drinking her bottle & patting my face, whispering "you feel better."

lori was crying in angel's arms as i laid kia in her bed. we held her & stroked her shoulders as she sobbed. later angel said he thinks i get all her anger because shes not afraid of losing me. & today, when she & i were walking to the library, she said "i take everything out on you. its not fair." she just ran in to tell me this halloween shes going to be peter pan; next halloween, tinkerbelle; & then wendy. i told her she was dressed like wendy now, cause wendy always flew to never never land in her nightie.

28.

well, so far the whole stay has been like that. one major tantrum each nite, first by kia & next nite by lori. each time i left the house for a few minutes to calm down & then called for help. its been a very bad week. (what about mothers who have no one to call for help? how do they survive?) dont know if there is any special reason for this week to be bad: except that i refuse to play martyr any more & am demanding a few things my own way, instead of constantly trying to indulge everyone else's needs & whims. & i've stopped acting as mediator between the kids & their fathers. (it hurts to hear them fight, but they *do* get thru them . . .)

the welfare money did not come yesterday; the worker did cut me off like she promised. but the medi-cal & foodstamps ($46 worth for $32) arrived. my first thot was "o good! i dont have to get married!"

feel crowded today. angel & the kids took care of themselves & i slept til 12:30. they did quite well without me! & i had no nitemares, so feel rested & healthy. for 2 months i've been dreaming disasters &

33

climbing stairs. but not last nite. so my skin is smooth & pink today & youd think i'd be glad to hop out of bed & wash dishes & be sociable. but i'm not. i want to sit in this back room, with the kids outside, & listen to the leaves bump around in the wind.

i had this great theory, is what it was. that i would write while the kids are here, since i'm writing about me & them. the material is at hand, so to speak. well forget it. i managed to forget, in my usual idealistic fashion, that one of the reasons our story is not told is that mothers have no time. i got to sleep late this morning, & that shot the wad. every minute since the kids got out here i have either been relating to someone (thank whoever there is to thank (me?) i dont live in a commune. when i did, with 13 people, each person would get angry at me for not relating to them each day! can you imagine trying to relate to 13 different people each *day?* i was on pain pills constantly for the migraine headache that cost) or cleaning house or recuperating. (recoup. hm.) i snatch quiet moments when i can, like all mothers i kno, but those stolen seconds do not create a book. books happen when you have time to think, time to form words, & most important of all, time to write those words down without simultaneously applying bandages, rinsing out bottles, wiping bottoms, picking scraps of paper off the floor, answering telephones, fixing food, & stopping quarrels. somehow i forgot that. (& somehow, i have managed the 4 minutes necessary to write these papagraphs altho the kids are right there in the front room & angel is asleep in the bedroom!) the kids singing along with ringo "ooh, i get by with a little help from my friends."

kia rode her trike into my workroom: "i came for visit you." lori was hiding from her in the closet, having admonished me not to tell cause she needed a bit of peace & quiet. kia said "i wanted to come for visit you but my brother wont let me."

"yr brother wont let you?"

"yeh. gregory is pretending for be my brother & he wont let me come for visit you." she rode around the room looking for the parking lot. "wheres lori?" i asked.

"shes hiding." answered kia. "in the closet." i stared at her & lori started laughing from behind the door, "o, that baby!" now theyre pretending that kia is the mommy & lori the baby. lori wants her bottom wiped cause she just went do do & kia is saying "but i'm at the gas station! & the car is locked! & i cant find my key!" lori suggests "well, pretend that the gas station is around the corner & that our house is just a couple of houses down, ok?"

"ok."

"come here, mommy! i did a do do!"

i love them so much. we're really happy when we're happy. i wish we could be happy all the time.

29.

a few days after christmas, a friend came out to visit. i was looking forward to it since she was the only adult i would have to talk to besides angel for more than a week. she drove out & we all sat at the table & i periodically had to get up & help the kids, during which times i would resent that the conversation went on without me since i was the one who needed it most. i had been out of the room for a few minutes washing up kia & when i returned to the kitchen, angel turned to me & said "ruth has been telling me about her sister in new york. she says sometimes during the winter there, she will be trapped in the apartment house for a week at a time because of all the snow & stuff."

i sat down silently.

ruth said "its true. i dont see how she can stand it. i would just go raving mad if i couldnt leave the house for days at a time."

i stared at them. they must be from another planet.

angel said "buns?"

i looked at them, realizing they really didnt know a thing about me, or about mothers, or what any of it is like, or that i had to leave the room constantly to attend to the children. i looked at each of them and i said "i have not stepped out of this house for 6 days."

30.

kia sang this & i wrote it down:

teddy bear, teddy bear, turn around.
teddy bear, teddy bear, turn around.
we'll turn you into butter

we'll turn you into butter
fly butterfly butterfly

> butterfly swings my wings
> butterfly swings my wings

i swinged my wings
i swinged my wings
all the way
up to the ceiling
& turned me back into
a teddy bear & the lil boy
who found me said "o!
my teddy bear again!"

& my butterfly turned back
into a butterfly & swinged her
wings up into the sky

31.

a hard thing. angel was practicing guitar behind me & i had to ask him to go to another room so i could concentrate. i would feel more comfortable if i shut the door, but i dont dare shut the door. i always feel the kids are more willing to understand those needs than other adults are. or maybe i just am not so afraid to hurt the children's feelings. adults so rarely understand. again this week, a woman i just met (we had been conversing for 3 hours) told me i didnt pay enuf attention to her. i just got mad & left. i cant deal with people like that. the kids at least can find entertainment elsewhere.

the neighborhood kids have torn a heavy branch on the fig tree. the fruit was so low even the 4 year olds could pick it without pulling down on the branches. i havent been letting the kids go back there because i didnt want the trees hurt, so of course, the kids snuck back there & took no care of the tree. i dont know how to handle it so i've ignored it. do i talk to the kids directly? i already did that. do i say "if you want figs, just ask. dont hurt the tree." (that might work.) i thot, of course, of ratting on them to their parents, but that creates 3 bad guys: me, for ratting; them, for sneaking into the yard; & their parents, who must punish them. and since the parents didnt kno they were sneaking into our yard (or they would have stopped them), what do they have to do with it anyhow? its not like they control the kids. my folks never controlled me, i just got sneaky. some things dont change.

there are enuf figs on it to feed the whole neighborhood. the only reason i didnt want the kids picking them was because i didnt want it hurt. maybe i'll go invite some of the kids to carefully pick the available fruit. (that is definitely not going to work. "how come lois gets to go & i dont?" "cause you might hurt the tree." "o, yeah?" that wouldnt solve anything. invite *all* the kids? & have one supervising older person to make sure they dont hurt the tree? gad, what a fiasco. invite the kids one at a time? & sit & watch them? & take away their figs if they do a no no? how did i get into this?)

i just shut the door.

32.

(retyping this, i stopped to read the rest of this section & forgot to put the pages in order. so they are no longer in the same order i wrote them. in order. as if my life were in order. who am i kidding.)

everyone was asleep by 11:00. & so i have had 3 hours to myself this week. one i spent writing letters; one, writing this; the other, i read poetry sent to me by women . . . 3 private hours in 6 days. i have had the snatches of solitude that most of us have: the minutes when everyone else is out of the house, or when we are alone in the yard. those moments. but the rest of the time i on call (indeed, am still on call: if the baby coughs, this paragraph will end) & altho this story, this very story that i am writing, that of being a mother, is going on, i have not had the chance to tell it. *that is why our story has not been told.* we can either live it or write it. we cannot do both simultaneously. & no one can write it who has not lived it.

& so i will have to wait until the children are again with their father before i can write these words that form in my head & disappear under folded towels. it is like swimming when the pool is dry.

& i think of the mothers who try: of sylvia plath, who rose at 4 each morning to write until her baby woke. of tillie olsen, who was

not published until she was 50, & her children all nearly grown. if
there are others to think of i hope i discover them. i need them all.

33.
nothing else is as beautiful as this:
nothing else fills yr eyes with the glory of it:
the face of yr child asleep.

34.
a poem came to me recently but it is gone. rachel nahem said she was
filled with aborted poems, poems that never had room to be born.
poems about her daughter that she needed to write, but there was no
way to write them.

so i had a poem recently; i cant remember when, or where, or what
it was about. i remember trying to hold on to it but the eggs were
done, or the tricycle was getting oil from the driveway on our carpet,
or the telephone rang. but i dont remember, really, what blew it; just
that it is gone. & i might have liked it, could i have written it.

i am writing this book because tillie said "our story has not been
told." i have been wondering, since everyone nags me to write a novel,
why i had no novel to write. but all it took was 6 words & the ready
book is flowing out of me like love. how simple are the keys that open
our hearts.

35.
i have loved children who grew up & went away. the foster kids. they
are all gone, & i have seen only 3 of them since they left me, 5 years
ago. only 3 of the 7, & each of them not more than twice. shawn
came to see me after the birth of her baby. she showed me a letter
from the people who had adopted it. she left home & stayed with me;
she lived with me 3 months & never told me she was pregnant.

i saw her on a bus last year: she was with a young man; they have
been living together happily & both going to college. she was on her
way to visit her father. she said to me "you look so old. i hardly
recognized you." & i watched her face & wondered if she had always
talked to me that way.

36.

tim had not finished hi school; in fact, he may not have finished junior hi. he was supposed to attend a special school for problem kids. as a good mother, i went with him & the p.o. to check out the school. tim acted up, climbing on the building, & so i tried to busy myself with talking to the girls. they were offered homemaking & typing. tim kept saying how proud of me he was that i visited there, but he never went back. (maybe i'm supposed to feel guilty? i dont.) anyhow, we decided his education was evidently going to have to take place at home. bo played chess with him & he learned car repair on his own (by lying on his back on the driveway under a car somebody gave him) & i asked him to read chaucer on tape for my father. dad loves dirty stories, & most books recorded for the blind (i typed "bland" by mistake, then realized thats how most people think of blind people) were religious, or readers digest type stuff. so tim took on the task of reading chaucer. bo & i were rather amazedly eavesdropping from the front room, hearing tim reading & guffawing into the tape recorder. there was a crash & we both stood up & tim ran from the bedroom, waving the book, "you hip to this cat absolem? man, the dude farts right in her old man's *face!*"

(as you can imagine, dad loved the tape, & tim was contracted to read 3 more books. if yr kid doesnt like to read, you might try giving her a dirty book.)

37.

not all of the kids we loved lived with us. some were fortunate enuf to have homes they were happy in. (does that sound self-righteous? it may be hard to be a foster mother & not come off sounding self-righteous.) one such kid was kevin. we met when lori & i were living here before, with bo. kevin was a friend of the paper boy's. they would come over for ping pong, monopoly, & to hang out. (now theres an odd expression.) whenever kevin had to make a decision in monopoly he would mutter "torn by doubt torn by doubt." now i'm 30 & kevin is 21 & we're still friends. he has not, as a matter of fact, changed much since we first met. he is heavily intellectual, soft spoken, conservative, & very funny. he saw the part about fuzzy fucker (chapter 16. shawn called him fuzzy fucker & i never did learn his "real" name.) & when he read that fuzzy had "grown up," kevin remarked "so yr peter pan!" (rereading that explanation, i see why bo went nuts when i told jokes. he even got mad that i laffed.) anyhow. during the last miscarriage, i had to be rushed to the doctor & i desperately searched my phone book for someone who could get me there. i called kevin & he raced over in tee shirt & jeans & stayed with me at the doctors altho angel had arrived by then· & could drive me home. angel had to return to work, & kevin spent the day here, straining to make conversation so that i would make it thru.

kevin never needed us for foster parents; he & his folks get along fine. many families are not so lucky. & there is not yet, in this society, adequate social support for those families. when parents need a rest, there is no where to go. when kids need another adult to turn to, they are lucky if there is a decent teacher (who they have to share with 35 other kids), for there is no other set-up for people of different ages to relate. so much has to be changed before our lives become even tolerable.

i just read that 4,000,000 more women have become addicted to tranquilizers this year. almost all of them are housewives. what are our alternatives? what do you do with the guilt, if you do not love all yr children? a friend told me yesterday the breakthru came for her when her lover said "relax! there is no rule that says you must love both your children! many women have kids they cant relate to. stop trying to force yr feelings. she left your body 11 years ago." and so dee did relax, & she found that she genuinely likes her daughter. they have never been close, & may never be; her daughter lives with other friends & they have both adjusted to that. if all adults loved children, if we loved all the children, the mismatched parents & kids could find relief, & love. if the children never had to wonder if they had a place to go. but so few people are willing to be mothers. so very few.

(i say that as a white woman in the united states, 1972. i kno it is not true everywhere.)

38.
today we returned home immediately after leaving & as i entered the house i heard crashing in the bedroom. i stormed in, & there was one of my favorite neighborhood boys, shamed & nervous. i demanded

40

"who else is in here?"

"nobody."

"thats a lie." i checked the windows. "howd you get in?"

"thru the window."

"the window is locked."

"the window in the other room." i checked & it was indeed open, altho i had not opened it today. i went back in the bedroom, yelled "get out of the closet!" p. repeated "theres no one else here."

"GET THE HELL OUT OF THE CLOSET!" r. fell thru the dresses, at my feet.

"get out of here & dont ever come back." they ran out. their sisters were visiting out front, undoubtedly saw them. i called angel. he said to tell their parents. i argued that their parents obviously had not put them up to it, & its between the boys & us. but later when i found angel's drawers had been ransacked, i felt littler than the occasion demands. our plan is to talk to the boys tomorrow: all 4 of us talk to them. hope it works. (as i wrote that i thot what the hell does that mean. & all day today i've hated boys as i saw them lounging on their streets.) & yesterday's paper announced that child beating has reached epidemic proportions: it is now the #1 cause of death among children in the good old u.s. of a. & angel said he couldnt understand that & the very next morning (today) he spanked kia because she wanted 3 pieces of bread for her sandwich.

lori just ran in "its leotard woman! well, actually, its leotard little girl!" & shes zooming around the front room, wonder woman style. good thing i dont have to solve all our problems. somebody out there helps me . . . & in the papers today (a month old, but what the hell, late literacy is better than il literacy) an article about children in china: how they share, & are very loving & affectionate. rather unlike frantic california. (but lori's comment when i told her: "thats what they *say* . . .")

& we sat eating dinner & there was a scraping on the house outside. i rose in my chair & lori said "probly just somebody moving their bike." but the noise happened again & i panicked: lori opened the curtains & there was gregory, scraping the windowsill with a hairbrush. "i'm cleaning yr house." he said thru the glass. kia was fascinated, took her chicken to the window to eat. greg called lori outside for a conference. He told her "tell kia to stop watching me. i feel stupid."

39.

well, we had our big meeting with r. & p. in the patio so i could hang up clothes. kia kept hitting them with large grasses she would pick & we would yell at her "stop hitting them!" & take away the grass & soon she'd be at it again . . . p. & r. told us the little kids had heard a burglar inside & asked them to investigate so they entered in thru the same window etc. angel said "is that the best story you can come up with?" & i said "i thot it was a pretty *good* story." lori angrily said "yr assuming theyre guilty! you cant assume theyre guilty!" she suggested i drive the same distance i had yesterday before returning to see if there would be time for the little kids to hear a burglar, notify r. & p. & all the rest. so i drove the same 3 blocks & while lori was timing me, the boys told angel they had really done it after all. but when lori & i joined them they busied themselves with professing their innocence. angel & i asked them what we should do & they said "tell our folks, i guess" & r. started crying about how he would get put on restriction if we did. kia by this time was no longer angry (nor were the rest of us) & was handing us all flowers. we did tell the mothers on the theory that we would want them to tell us if our kids went in their houses uninvited . . . & i'm glad thats done with & i hope its done with.

40.

what is it like in china. why dont the kids fight there. would anyone get mad if they saw a neighbor in their house? would a neighbor *go* in their house? maybe lori's right & the kids fight there too, we just dont hear about it.

41.

thinking about why i was so happy those 4 months. because i was a true believer. & that takes away so much of the strain. considering becoming a jesus freak again (see section 24) just so i can spiritually rot. but for those 4 months i believed in that alternative school (kids would no longer have to take stupid tests, kiss up to teachers, go to classes they hated; girls could take any subject they wanted . . . the world would be new); i believed in poetry (i knew that everytime i read my work, everyone within earshot would be spellbound. & they were. it is no longer true.); i believed in love (when i was with bob i didnt even notice other men; couldnt have told you who was handsome & who was not & i thot the same was true for him & we would sail off into the sunset & true love was no lie even lifetime love made sense); & i believed in the women's movement.

(o, god, i sit here so ragged at the edges, slumped over the typewriter. i wish i could be innocent again. but at 31—& after all that—whatever could i believe was greater than me again, could redeem me? nothing. nada. & the men involved in watergate so believing: porter saying "my loyalty to this man goes back longer than any person that you will see . . . i have loved this man since i was 6 years old, & he shook my hand." maybe its just as well i recognize no higher authority.)

the women's movement was going to make it so that my children would never have to go thru what i went thru. no more rapes. no more marriages. no more years of being trapped in a house, unable to speak to adult men other than my husband, & adult women because they were all waiting in *their* houses & besides they all wanted to steal my husband so we didnt dare be friends no more of that. & then getting kicked off the *babe* (the first women's newspaper). they said "you threaten our identity." & the women's movement was no stronger than all the trapped, ghetto-ized american white women i was surrounded by. they were angry, they were afraid, & they knew they wouldnt have to go to jail if they took it all out on me so they took it all out on me. i may have been hurt that deeply in my life before, but that nearly killed me. in fact, i may have lost all those beliefs in that one year (1970). i got kicked out of that school by the director because i was sick of volunteerism & demanded a salary (the only paid woman staffer was the secretary) & he was surrounded by willing scabs. he didnt need me. bob didnt want just me: he wanted to find another woman so he could watch us eat each other. people read my poetry & then trashed each other just like in the old days & the war hasnt stopped & women still get married . . . & women learning how to fight too often only fight each other. the hell with it all. & so i moved back to san lorenzo.

42.
lori sang this song:

i feel so good
but i dont know why
i'm just a lettle thing
but i feel so high

doo doo doo
doo doo
doo doo doo

i'm just a lettle thing
but i feel so high

43.
another page. just sitting here, tired, waiting for the words to stop &
i'll go to bed (i dont want the words to stop! no! but it is late, & i will
have to get up tomorrow: angel leaves for work at 5:30 again) & so i
choose fatigue because i want these pages; i want the words to pour
out like love; i want to release all the years, the days, the mornings &
evenings, the afternoons when i wait for evening. i want to release it &
live it. i want you to know what it is like.

what it is like is the children sleeping in their room, the vaporizor
going to help them breathe; angel sleeping in our bed, waiting for me
even in his sleep so that when i go to bed he will reach out for me; this
lamp on the desk that i bought from the kids next door for 75¢ & just
got a 3 way bulb that really works & the phony corrective type to
cover up typos but it doesnt work too good & i cant keep stopping for
the sake of good housekeeping / my chair is breaking. its wicker &
secondhand & the right half of my ass is decidedly lower than the left
half. & its late & i'm tired & i'm happy because i love to write even
when i'm bitching & because i love the kids even when i feel crowded.
thats what its like.

there are more words, i could do this for days, but i am now so
tired that i just read the last paragraph & then noticed my eyes were
shut so i hope the next time i have time, the words will come.

44.

i have heard two women this month say their bodies are starting to look like their mother's. & so they are exercising desperately. desperately trying to deny the final proof of what we are.

45.

in 1965 there was a celebration ball for the homosexual community, a new years ball with leading clergy & assorted celebrities. i was incarcerated as a housewife in san lorenzo, just 20 miles from san francisco, & i knew nothing about it.

at about that same time, jack spicer was giving readings in berkeley. i had never heard of jack spicer, & now hes dead.

i sat in my house, & loved my daughter, & cared for her, & we sat in our house away from the world & had only each other & were very lonely. i will never live like that again.

46.

kia said today "momma takes care of me in the dark."

yesterday lori & i read 4 chapters of the nancy drew mystery *the mystery of the moss covered mansion.* that was the first nancy drew i had ever seen. marla showed it to me on the rare nite i was allowed to stay at her house all nite. we read it in her dark room, with her folks asleep, by light from a flashlite, & we got *scared*! 23 years later, lori & i read the first chapter in broad daylite with kia sitting by us demanding "read this book! read this book!" waving *the wizard of oz* at us. as i say, lori & i read it in broad daylite, with kia for company, & we got *scared*!

kia climbed up next to me while i was reading to myself on the bed & she said "is this san nerenzo?"

"yeh."

"wheres tuesday?"

47.

how can i ask somebody how to write this book. how come the first 11 pages happened with scarcely an interruption & the rest have been so unpredictable? writing this is like trying to plan things with the kids. i have what i think is a great plan (a picnic, say) & it turns out a total fiasco. or i set aside 2 hours to write & everything is either not worth mentioning, or would take 10 hours. virginia woolf called her books her children.

angel says the book is already written, altho to me it feels like just the title of a poem. just sketches / but thats what he meant. heres the sketch—could i do a whole portrait?

(but what to tell? there are already so many anecdotes in these 47 chapters: surely not more anecdotes? its not done, i *know* its not done, i've barely scratched the surface! poetry seems easier. you just capture the essence; you dont have to relate the daily details. & the pain, tho intense, just lasts the length of the poem. raising kids is both poetry & prose. thats why the story is just begun. no matter how much i write.)

this book is the photograph of a woman giving birth.

momma: book II

momma: book II

1.

there are many kinds of mothers. & there are many situations you can
find yourself in. the ones i've seen are: nuclear family (one dad plus 1
mom plus kids), extended family (nuclear plus grandparents or aunts,
uncles etc. either in the home or nearby), divorced nuclear (one
parent plus kids), substitute parents (grandparents who take the role
of parent; foster parents, etc.) & none (kids in institutions). i have
formed no clear conclusions about any of them, except the kids i
knew when i was growing up were both happy & sad, & my mom
tended to disapprove of those who did not live with their parents
(they said dirty words maybe?) & the only really messed up ones were
those who had been abandoned. but those same messed up kids have
grown up to be fine adults. so where does that leave us & what does it
prove?

there were so many who grew up with their mom in their bed. she
would sleep with the kid instead of the husband. when i was a child,
that seemed particularly perverse to me. & i kicked mom out when
she tried it. but so many of the women in her generation refused to
sleep with their mates. (4 years ago my brother called "hey! i just
heard this great idea! joan baez (i think) said women should refuse to
screw soldiers & then the war would end!" i answered, "i got an even
better idea. women should refuse to screw men & then sexism would
end!" i did quit, too, but after that mess with the *babe* i could hardly
believe in revolutionary feminism so now i take whatever i can get.)

another part of what i saw as our mother's perversion was that so
many slept with their sons. but last week i think i may have figured
out why. i was mad at angel & didnt want to go to bed since he was in
it, so when i got tired i went to the other bed, which had the kids in
it. i lay down next to them & watched them sleep for awhile, which
always overwhelms me with love since nobody is doing a no no &
they look so lovely, & i thot "too bad i cant sleep in here. if it

48

wouldnt give the girls a trauma, i would. then angel could eat his heart out all night heh heh." then i listened to what i'd said & all the women who slept with their kids flashed thru my head. all but one have been with the same husband all their lives. divorce is out of the question, evidently. how to effectively divorce yr husband but still get room & board? sleep with the kids. he cant accuse you of adultery cause yr not doing it. he cant raise hell, it would traumatize the children. he cant accuse you of desertion cause youve only walked across the hall. & he cant fuck you in front of the kid. all he can do is lie there lonesome while you rest comfortably, undisturbed by his horny lil cock.

now maybe this is not why all those mothers did it, but it definitely *is* why i almost did it. (tillie, who has had years more to learn with than i have, read this & said *"because they were afraid of getting pregnant!* thats why, after menopause, so many couples have a second honeymoon!")

there were probably happy couples among the parents i knew, but i wouldnt have given any prizes. my pal betty in reno lived with a foster mother, along with 4 or 5 other kids. she saw her mother periodically & seemed content with the arrangement. her foster mother really loved the kids. betty had a little brother that she was very fond of. he lived with their mother but betty didnt seem to resent that. (writing that, i remembered ann olly, as betty called her. she was plump & white & smiled hello to me & kept the aspirin up hi.)

i was jealous of some of my california friends. judy had a mom who did all the mom type things. she dressed like a mother, she made cookies all the time, she laughed indulgently when judy swooned over elvis presley & she talked to judy honestly about everything, including menstruation. what more could a daughter ask? but i have no idea if she was happy. altho she had been married to the same man for 17 years, she still slept with him. that seemed like a good sign.

& in between those mothers were all the others: the divorced, the frequently remarried, the ones who disappeared into woodwork, the runaways. & i knew which one i wanted to be. i wanted to be judy's mother. i learned to make peanut butter cookies on purpose: i even wore an apron. but something went amiss. i turned out to be one of those frequently remarried mothers.

49

2.

i went thru agony deciding to divorce bo. what would it do to lori? all the propaganda about broken homes, children of divorce. she had begun to say "daddy, mommy, baby. we are a family!" with all the careful pronunciation of her 2½ years. i had tried singlehanded to hold that marriage together & i didnt want to anymore. but what right had i to cop out? to choose my own happiness at the expense of my child? i had to find out if it would be at her expense. i talked to everyone, i read everything i could get my hands on (including dozens of "can this marriage be saved?" one of which helped tremendously: in the end, the wife promises to stop daydreaming so much & spend more time on housework. i was not going to die like that for a man i no longer loved. come to think of it, i was no longer going to die like that even for a man i *did* love!) & what i learned from all those conversations & all that reading was that there were worse things in a child's life than divorce. & living in a loveless home was one of them.

but i still wonder if there could have been another way to do it. maybe i should have done it sooner (how could i have done it sooner? all my life i had waited to be that, how could i quit just because it was no good?) well, maybe i could have stopped bo from ever seeing her, so that now it wouldnt hurt that he never comes to see her. but how did i kno he would walk out of her life? even he could not be *that* cold. obviously i misjudged.

argh. i dont want to write about all this. its too ikky. any woman who has found herself in love with a man will understand all too well. who needs explanations?

(how can a man be no good? how can anyone be no good? my idealistic adrenalin starts revving: theres no such thing as a bad boy . . . o yeh? then where do all these husbands come from?)

3.

& so to father number 2. i passed over an incredible line-up to live with simon. a rich physicist who showered lori with presents, assorted students, a cab driver who might very well have been devoted, & another poet. i picked simon cause i liked his poems & cause he was cute. i never considered how he would be as a father. he was probably the very worst i could have picked. he was frantically jealous of her:

50

he would yell at her when she cried & he would spank her whenever she stepped over his arbitrary, self-indulgent lines. she changed from a delightfully happy, loving child to a frightened little girl. & i was part of that change.

i followed his line, somehow. i yelled at her not to suck her thumb. i yelled at her when she spilled milk (which she did every dinnertime). i never thot of solutions to these problems, like buying a spillproof cup, i just kept on yelling. i was miserable, & how could i put her thru yet another divorce? better i kill myself. so i kept a calendar; after each day i would write yes or no, whether or not that day was worth living thru. at the end of the alloted 100 days, i counted. a majority of nos meant suicide. 49 nos, 51 yesses.

but still i did not consider divorce. we stuck it out for 3 arduous years. the boggler was, simon & i love each other & are great friends. we just should *nev*er live together! finally, kia was born so lori & i had company. & i rediscovered an old friend & decided to live with her instead.

(here i must say that simon has changed. he loves lori now & is good with her; & he insists on having the children half the time. he had to learn to love, but he did learn. is learning.)

4.

well. its bad enuf going thru 2 husbands. its bad enuf living with just 1 parent. what could possibly be harder on the kids?

how about living in a home with one gay parent & her lover? if i suffered guilt over the other situations, you can imagine this question was just so big i wouldnt deal with it. lo & behold, the other kids i saw from gay homes were no worse off than those from heterosexual homes. i used to think people could tell if i failed as a mother if my kid turned out queer. but now what if i turned out queer? (i neednt have worried, of course. kids are so willing to understand: so willing to let you grow too.) the only reaction i ever noticed from them was when lori walked in on me & dena lying in each others arms. she yelled "mother! what are you doing?"

& i answered "dena & i are doing lovins."

lori shook her head, grinned embarrassedly, "thats silly." end of question & answer period.

51

we did try a camping trip. doesnt that sound familial & summery? well, shit. a total fiasco. first we drive to this public campground & find a spot to sleep. looks ok, not too far from the pot. we get sort of settled & our neighbors return. a family full of loud beer drinking men. & we are 5 women: 2 adults & 3 kids. lions & lambs.

the girls wanted to go swimming. thats fine, i love to swim. so we walk to the river. a mile & a half. all the good nature they had stored up for the trip began to wear thin. "wheres the river?"

"lets go back & get the car." bitch, bitch. but we got there & got wet. so far so good. some super american fatty with a football is terrorizing his little boy *"catch* it! *catch* it! whats the matter with you?"

lori, naturally, could not stand to see the boy treated like that & began to help him retrieve the football, slipping it to him & saying "dont worry about what yr daddy says." & his dad started raving "for gods sake dont let that *girl* catch the football! dont you have any *pride?"*

so after our pleasant swim, trudge trudge back to camp. the girls are hungry & we wouldnt buy them cotton candy & popcorn on the theory that we would have a great time with barbecued hotdogs back at camp.

we built a fire: that part wasnt hard, dena & i had both been girl scouts. but we had never had 3 people yelling at us "cook, already!" "we cant cook yet. we have to get the fire just right."

"whats wrong with the fire?"

"*no*things wrong with the fire, its just not ready to be cooked on!"

step 2: no hot dogs. what happened to the hot dogs?

step 3: cook potatoes instead.

"wheres our hotdogs?"

"we cant find them."

"whaddya mean, you cant find them? you told us we were gonna eat hot dogs!"

dena is busily peeling potatoes. i pull out a can of peas. "canned peas?!" yells one of the girls. "for canned peas, we could have stayed home!" dena & i look at each other. now theres an idea. she drops the potatoes in the finally boiling water. as she turns to get a fork, she bumps the handle of the pan. it tips; the potatoes fall in the fire & the

52

water nearly puts it out. we eat cold smokey peas.

we are all hungry; we're tired. the girls are yelling "you cant just feed us canned peas, mother! at least buy us some cotton candy!"

dena & i sit down wearily on the tarp. we stare at the sleeping bags. the girls plow thru the car, unearth some potato chips. "what do you spose happened to the hot dogs?" i ask. dena says "i bet those finks ate em."

the beer drinking males start to sing "fuck em all! fuck em all! fuck the long & the short & the tall . . ." one of them stands up & walks behind a tree, unzips his pants & pees. we are also behind the tree. about 8 feet away. dena turns away in disgust. the girls freeze in fascination. "hey, psst!"

dena gets up, throws the sleeping bags into the car, & sits behind the wheel. the girls say "now what?" & she says quietly, "get in." so we pick up the tarp, the cokes & bowls, & get in the car & drive home. we stopped in a restaurant on the way home & that was as bad as the camping trip. her oldest child decided that everything i said should be repeated. even the other kids didnt think it was funny. we ate in silence.

but lori & kia weathered the camping trip, just as they weathered my love affairs & marriages & moving & flipping out. i look at least 30 all the time now, but they still love me.

5.

i just showed lori this last story & asked her if she remembered anything else about the camping trip. "well," she mused, "i do remember wanting to eat a raw hot dog . . ." my mouth dropped open. "i probly didnt eat it, tho. no, probly i didnt eat it."

6.

i used to do everything i could think of to stop the war. periodically i would go to draft boards & talk to the men going in. one of the signs i carried said SUPPORT THE WAR. BEAT YR KID.

7.

kia got wet playing in the bathroom basin & i came in to change her dress. she looked up, "i got all wet. you sposed to get mad at me."

"i'm sposed to get *mad* at you?"
"yes! "
"what am i sposed to do to you?"
"you sposed to *yell* at me!"
lori had been calling mady "aunt mady" all day. when kia went for
her nap, i asked her to first kiss mady nite nite. kia refused, saying
"shes ikky. shes a ant."

california / 1972

i walk past those homes
& hear the
mothers striking the
children

      (i am one of those
      mothers
      striking
      the children)

& the screams, the screams
of us trapped animals
striking one another
& screaming

& screaming

      *

i stand outside,
uncertain;
should i knock
& offer myself?
or would it only shame them,
frighten them,
would they hit each other harder.
& would they hate me,
besides.

so i have turned the corner
& can no longer hear the screams.

(o yes you can!)

I CAN NO LONGER HEAR THE SCREAMS!

8.

kia telling us a nite nite story: once upon a time there was alice, & she
didnt wonder.

i told lori & angel i figured out why i'm a "natural leader." its
cause everyone thinks i kno where i'm going, so they follow me. lori
said "thats cause you tell them you kno where yr going. like now."

today on the bus, kia turned to the woman next to her & said "you
black?"
"yes."
"why you black?"
the woman touched kia on the arm & asked "why are you *that*
color?"
kia stared at her own arm, then pointed at me. "thats my mommy.
shes blue."
i opened my mouth, glanced around at the bus full of amused people,
& said "you mean i have blue eyes."
kia shook her head. "no, you got a whole blue head."

9.

the overwhelming love. their faces so soft; i lie next to them as they
sleep & all my horror dissolves: all the anxiety of trying to live free in
this country reduces itself, bows to the love

i tucked kia in & lay next to her, warming her after changing her
wet clothes, & i kissed her on her baby cheek & she turned her face to
me & puckered her lips in a kiss, still asleep. her eyes shut, the
lashes—i rest. & touch her face & wish her no harm. i reach over to
take her sister's hand & slowly i calm down, i rest. the overwhelming
love that wishes them no harm. i want the world to be safe & happy
just so they can be safe & happy. nothing is worth killing any body
for.

they sigh as i stroke their hair. they know how i love them. i could love all the children now; all the children. my heart is so full.

10.

i get up late partly so that the kids cant get mad at me. lori goes to school 5 days of the week, so i get up just before she leaves, to keep up the appearance of motherhood, & so that she doesnt have long to yell at me. she did manage, while i was still in bed; kia was singing & lori was yelling at her to shut up so i yelled at lori to let kia sing & lori swooped in my room & screamed "you dont like it when she whines in yr face, do you?" i had been planning to get up soon but after that i decided there was no point in it, so i got back under the covers. at 9:40 i got up & we said goodbye & she left at 9:43. that left me & kia. we can make it for hours sometimes, without a fight. so i figured today we would dress coolly & go out in the patio. she could blow bubbles & i could decide how to feel. so we went in the bathroom where i had to clean off her bottom cause she shits in her diapers every morning. i nagged her why doesnt she go in her potty cause its so much easier & she replied, as she always does, "i wanted to go in my didies." after i washed her i cut her nails & asked her to wash her hands. she said she didnt want to. i told her to do it anyway. she said she didnt want to. i yelled "wash yr hands!" & she yelled "i dont want to!" so i screamed "wash them wash them wash them" & by that time i was in tears. she started to cry, her hands under the water "i dont want to!" so i went in the bedroom & got my clothes & told angel, who was trying to sleep thru it all since i kept him up til 2 last night fighting, i told him "i'm going out."

he muttered from under the covers "ok." but i went in & took a shower instead. as i was drying, kia came out from her room where she had been crying & yelling "i hate you." she came into the bathroom & looked up at me. "you not sad anymore?"

i looked at her—she is almost up to my hips now—& said "i'm not so sad." she smiled. "i'm not so sad as i was. you was sad cause i didnt want to wash my hands & i was sad cause i didnt want to wash my hands."

"yes, buns."

11.

now i'm in the back room typing. i have an hour & a half, then angel leaves. it's his day off, but he has to get glass for the back window which someone thru an apple thru, & hes going to visit a friend. he figured we would all go, but hes leaving at 1:00 & lori is in school til 3:00. so kia & i will stay home, then lori & kia & i will stay home.

yesterday some woman said they would come at 3:00 so i waited all day for them & stayed home altho we needed the glass & i wanted to go to the post office. they didnt come. not only did they not come, they did not call to say they would not come, nor did they call later to apologize. while i was showering today, i planned responses if they ever come by.

say she arrives: we have never met; she is just the friend of a friend. but a woman we both know said she also wanted to come & so would drive her to my house. say they show up today. i answer the door & she gushes "o! its so good to meet you finally!" & tries to hug me. i stand immobile & when they back off i say "i waited for you yesterday & you didnt come. i dont want to see you because i dont like being treated like that." they say "but we drove 20 miles just to see you!" i say "you should definitely get something for all your trouble." i shut & lock the door, get some scrap paper, make a circle & write HERO in it, then open the door & hand it to them. i say "here" & shut the door. then i hear 20 different versions of my snotty behavior next time i go to the city.

12.

simon kept screwing other women while we were together. his dad wanted him to be a professor & i'd think jeez, thats all i need. but women follow simon like bees do purty little flowers, so there was no where for me to go but out. in the midst of one of his affairs i thot, fuck it, why should i stay home when theres a world full of men out there—& i began my strategy by calling an old lover who was one of my favorites. we had had a great time in bed, & enjoyed each others company as well. he had worked out the troubles with his wife & last i heard, they were together. but there wasnt anybody else i wanted, so i called him at work. a guy answered & said he wasnt there & i should call his house & i said i didnt think i should, actually, & he said "o. i see. well, you want to leave yr name & i'll tell him you called? but he doesnt work here anymore, see." so there was nothing for it finally but to call him at home. luckily it was a long distance call so his wife only talked to the operator. but when i told him who it was, he was so surprised, he shouted my name. his wife *must* have heard that. i always get caught when i screw out. how come everybody else can get away with it but me? so i assume he had to explain a bit to his wife. anyhow, we met, & he drove me to the hills. just our luck there were family picnics behind every bush. simon used to take women to the hills to fuck all the time. everytime *i've* tried it, the goddamn girl scouts are on a nature hike. so we were stuck in the car, one hour to do it, & we did our best. but of course i couldnt relax, & he actually knew i didnt come. most men didnt care, & couldnt tell anyway, but he could (which is one reason we were good together). i tried to fake it, but he knew, & he said "o, come on, baby, dont lie. lets go get a room & i'll try to make it better for you." but i was due home, so that was that. another problem is that he refused to wear rubbers, so i had to pack foam. i usually miscarry, so i didnt plan ahead for birth control.

i had decided to leave simon & get an apartment with just me & lori, or something, but he talked me into taking a trip with him first. a month of travel might bring us together. part of it was nice, actually; especially vancouver & a lovely camp in washington. the rest was crappy. & while in vancouver, i went to the doctor to see why my belly felt funny. i was pregnant. she advised no sex, no travel, bed rest: the usual advice i get when i'm pregnant & bleeding. by the time we had returned to california, the bleeding had stopped & i felt in no position to find a place for lori & me. so the 3 of us got a house. while we were waiting for a house, we stayed with some friends & i realized that he had screwed the woman we were staying with. i went beserk, as could be expected, & during the fight later i was running down the street & he was trying to stop me so that we wouldnt lose the baby & i screamed "i wish you didnt know if this was your child!" he got me back home, & when we were calmer, asked me what i had meant. so i told him. he was shocked & hurt, & the question then became: do we go thru with the pregnancy or get an abortion? if it were not his child, & the grandparents got all worked up & then saw a brown baby, we could hardly say it was his child. there was no way to fake it. & there was no way to know, for 7 months, what color the child would be.

so after some agony, we decided to keep the kid & let the grandparents fall where they wished. but things are never quite as i plan them. the 3 months went by fairly uneventfully, & i was told the danger of miscarriage was past, & i had dinner with some women friends & told them how we (the baby & i) were doing fine. then i went home, fixed lori's bed, started bleeding, & 16 hours later lost the child. it splashed out all over the doctors chest. & he cleaned me out, then stood by me & took my hand & there were tears in his eyes too & i said "i kind of wanted that baby" & he said "i know you did."

i dont want to write about this anymore.

13.

i woke at 5 with angel, & tho we only had a few hours sleep, i am wired. thinking about lori, about being a parent, about how her father has deserted her & how the hell is a kid supposed to handle something like that. adults cant handle rejection: what are kids supposed to do? maybe he is doing it because his father did it to him: his father never helped much with the kids after the divorce. but we must *break* these chains! we cannot allow past pain to rule our love relationships.

& so i sermonize to myself, for hours & hours, hating her weak father (is he weak?), hating her lying father, hating him. she can certainly understand now why i divorced him. but what good does that do her? i can feel righteous; she doesnt even have that consolation.

last nite she was crying & wouldnt say why. i sat on her bed, insisting she tell me, wondering what bruno bettleheim would think of my tactics, what dr. spock would advise, what karen horney has observed about kids with one natural parent & where their anger goes, & thinking how futile it is to consult psychiatrists when there are no rules for this game. there is no way to prepare a human being for rejection or desertion of one parent. there is no way to make up for it. i see it as an act of malice & so do the kids. survival, is what the deserting parent calls it. they had to leave the kids, their mate, the situation or whatever for their survival. ok. but after they have survived, youd think they could care about the kids again. unless they are dead. & so her father is dead, somewhere; he feels guilt periodically, & writes her about how he feels bad that he hasnt written her for so long, & he'll certainly do better in the future, & he loves her, & thats the last she hears from him until we call him again & . . . . & what? nag him to write? ask how he is? what is it called, what we do? she calls him because she cant stand to go without him completely. i handle the call because it is long distance & operators freak out when kids make calls. i dont tell him what i think of him, altho there is no doubt as to what i do think of him. i hate him. he is a coward, a liar, he has no more guts than any other deserting father; if he left for his own survival, he now has his own survival (as much as any white poor man in this country) & he damn well ought to care about his kid. my kid. our kid? lori.

but what i was thinking about was how i enlisted lori's help in capturing simon. he was a traveler, & i wanted him to stop travelling & commit himself to us. one of the first steps was to ask lori to call him daddy john. dig it. this guy spanks her for no good reason, yells at her, has lived with us for 3 weeks & i convince her to call him daddy john. so he wont leave us. i wouldnt do that now, of course. but i hadnt discovered the women's movement then (1967). i hadnt read *the feminine mystique* because i didnt know what *mystique* meant. i figured that book was just another tell me how to save my marriage trip. & all the women i knew were such sellouts that they were horrified that i would even divorce bo, for christ's sake. so i used my feminine wiles to keep us alive & taught lori how to do that too. immediately.

to keep us alive? did i really think we would die without simon? its possible. i was so fucked up.

i thot last nite "your first kid is to make mistakes with" & realized that sounds a lot like "wombs are to suffer with." but it helps with the guilt, anway; we all do make mistakes with our kids; maybe more mistakes with the first, since we dont know what the hell we're doing. the nuclear family is no good. sociologists write books about that. in the meantime i've got this kid who was part of our nuclear family & her dad has split & i love her & dont want her to cry at night especially when she feels she cant tell me why, & what alternative is there? i've tried a few & *none of them worked*! meantime, her father is surviving on a farm in oregon with his new wife & their kids. i hope to hell he doesnt treat those kids like he treats lori. nobody deserves to be treated like that.

14.

i guess lori crying like that is her latest attempt to deal with that pain. we havent really had one of our drag out fights this week, altho the night before, we did get into a slight tantrum. i figured there were one per visit, after that one, since i have to figure something. (& have since realized that i am more strict, more protective, than their other pair of parents so every shift from them to us the kids have to learn again our limits since theyre changing as the kids are growing) & the tantrums seem to happen the first night the kids return here. but lori didnt scream how she hates me & wants to "go home" (me: wheres home? her: how should i kno?). & last nite, she just cried, without calling me names. i guess thats part of her new knowledge that she takes everything out on me, as she told me when we walked to the library, remember? well, people do that. i used to take everything out on her. angel says now i take it all out on him. i wonder if thats progress. (i wonder if thats true.)

i sat with the children after they fell asleep again last night. i was going to write "they sure are easy to love, when theyre asleep." but somehow that sounds immoral.

as i touched lori's face, i flashed on her as a baby: she was so strong! 2 weeks early, 9 pounds 4 ounces, she could lift her head the very first day! & in the photo they took 24 minutes after her birth, she is smiling. nobody had ever seen a happier child. she used to giggle as she fell asleep; she never hit other children (altho she was slow to share, as many first kids are in this country). she wasnt afraid of adults: just an incredibly happy baby. but shes getting acclimatized. how much did i have to do with that. how much is because of her father. how much is just this world. the war. all our filthy habits.

why couldnt everyone who saw her join in her joy? why did her father go.

i sit at the desk, my head in my hands, my mouth turned down. in that posture i have seen my mother in, so many times. shes a friggin tornado, making a world on little else than her own will, but every now & then she would just fold. just sit with her head in her hands, the lines deep in her face. & i worried about how she didnt wear aprons & make peanut butter cookies. i've always been a very deep person.

the sun is almost up. i'm tired, but not a bit sleepy. guess i'll go make some tea. kia is stirring; she'll probly wake soon. tonite angel's folks are coming over. his mom is a whole nother story.

(i may go to sleep after lori wakes up. i always feel more secure when shes up: i figure the weight is off me a little bit, & i can rest.) i thot i heard kia padding around on her little feets, but shes quiet now. i'm gonna go get my agatha christie & make tea. if i dont fall asleep on the way to the kitchen. looks like its gonna be a really pretty day.

15.

yes. well. the kids watched tv for a couple of hours & i rested in bed, mostly reading my book. off to rhodesia, to live on an island with her rogish lover, surrounded by revolutions. sort of the life i've tried to create for myself, here in a california suburb. of course, this suburb is not exactly an island, & we do not live without money worries, but what the hell. we cant all be displaced english people in the heart of beautiful africa in 1922.

the kids & i went shopping & had mostly a lovely time, & on the way back i was doing my best w.c. fields impersonation & the kids were laffing & all of a sudden lori was screaming STOP IT STOP IT you made my stomach hurt from laffing so i thot gee thats nice but she was still screaming / i mean for real. it lasted like that for 2 blocks. i picked kia up out of the shopping cart & set her down to walk, with a box of shredded wheat. you can maybe picture it now: lori 20 paces in front of me, sniffling, with occasional bursts of "very funny!" me in the middle, pushing a very heavy shopping cart full of tonites dinner & the weeks supplies, kia, 20 paces behind me yelling "i dont wanna walk! i dont wanna walk!" if the neighbors saw us, they politely pretended they didnt.

when we got home, both kids were still crying, so i said "i intend to be happy today, & since you guys want to be miserable, you will do it outside." they of course screamed at me about how they didnt want to go outside, but i was adamant. i've never done that before,

62

altho most other mothers i know do; i've always considered it a little hard nosed. but recently i have decided that i am entitled to my share of happiness, too. that i dont want to be anybody's sacrificial lamb, whether as artist, woman, wife or mother. fuck em all. i want to be happy.

so i put the groceries away, then sat in the rocker listening to jazz, & read. in walks kia, with a shy smile: "i not crying any more." lori is right behind her. "hi" says lori. i turn to say hi but kia is shoving lori out the door & shutting it. i tell her to let lori in but lori had decided to run away. kia informs me "she gonna run away." i tell her to go get lori & ask her to have lunch with us but kia refuses, "she gonna run away." finally she agrees to get lori but comes back with the message "she ran away."

so i mumble around for awhile, decide maybe we all need a foster home, then start to worry. what if lori really does try to get somewhere? & all mothers worry about the evil men walking the street / i panic & go out & yell for lori. no answer, of course. i console myself that everybody else's kids run away, & i used to do it all the time. a few minutes later lori comes in the back door & sits on the couch & cries. i think "i am staying home for the good of the children." she calms down & joins me in the kitchen. as we eat lunch, i realize that instead of us relating beautifully for 12 hours a day when i stay home, they just have more time to yell at me with. after lunch i send them outside again. kia cries "i dont wanna go outside! i not sad anymore!" but i'm determined. & i sit in the house, watching them play on the grass, & think, they dont need me 12 hours a day. they need someone to care for them, & they need playmates & things to do, but for all the good times we have, a couple of hours a day would do it. the cloud of guilt over my head begins to fade, muttering "you cant get away with it!" but i'm not listening anymore. there is nothing to get away with. the kids do not need me 12 hours a day. & i dont need to be yelled at, anymore.

16.

what is it like to be the oldest child. to have a younger sister with curly, golden hair that everyone says is so darling & listens to what she says. when angel's folks came tonite, one of the first things they said was how pretty kia's hair looked, all brushed. lori went to the bathroom & brushed her hair. she came out, brush in hand, & listened to us talk. after dinner she brushed her hair some more. but nobody told her she has gorgeous hair.

i remember dad playing with my brother. i remember standing in the middle of the room, watching them, & wanting to be on his lap. when i was a teenager, mom finally told me dad was afraid to rough-house with me because i was a girl. so i went out with big men who would hold me on their laps. it wasnt exactly the same thing.

(as i wrote that, i remembered sitting in the back seat of a car, another couple next to us. i was on some big man (well, he was probly 18, anyway) & he was rubbing my back, feeling the rough cotton dress; touching, touching my back. i nestled into his shoulder. & peered out at the world, feeling vaguely secure. i was pretty big myself, by then: 5'5" & 130 pounds. but he didnt complain about me being heavy on his lap.)

17.
i saw my children as oppressors monday. the principal of lori's school ratted on us to the truant officer—why was this child only attending school half time? because we, her parents, have joint custody, & she lives here half time. well, she cant. well, she does. well, have a cop. so after the truant officer's visit (except that he wasnt really here; his mouth came but his head & ears stayed out in the car) i marched to the principal's office monday. to tell him what i thot of him. he saw me coming & called the truant officer to protect him (i could see him calling, looking frightened, thru his venetian blind) & told his secretary to keep me out til the officer got there. i sat down, thot "i didnt come here to see mouth again" & burst into his office. "you are afraid to face me alone after what youve done. but you *will* face me!" we didnt get much farther when the officer arrived. angel came, too, & we watched the mouth mouth for awhile, then the mouth left & the principal carried on about disturbed children, being very careful to explain that he knew lori was an excellent student & caused the school no trouble, & maybe something could be worked out. angel & i could approach the legislators to change the law. we went to her teacher, after, & lori was present for that talk. her teacher was, naturally, upset, since she likes lori & sees no harm in the situation. so

64

the next morning, lori's teacher from last year & the one from this year went to the principal, showed him some of lori's work, & demanded that he allow her to stay as a part time pupil. he called me an hour later.

"i've called off the dogs. i feel you & i can work this out, & lori should be able to continue." i told him that was good. he continued "you have a lot of friends at this school." & i thot again of how powerless we are, against all their rule books & robes, but we have, even when we have nothing, we have more than they do: we have our lives, & people who believe in our right to live those lives. i had no faith that we would win this fight. no conscious faith, anyway. its a revelation to win a fight. & i always wonder if its better to get hassled & fight & win or to be let alone, to live in peace. winning is really a trip. but it certainly is easier, is less pain, to be let alone in the first place.

so, you can imagine, after all that i was exhausted. &, as often happens when people are exhausted, we all turned on each other. i was the most convenient scapegoat.

18.

i went to see daddy today cause hes sick & he told me this story: he was tuning a piano in a bar in reno & when he got it all put back together, a woman came up & mumbled "play melancholy baby." & shoved $2 in his hand. he tried to explain that he only tuned pianos, but she had wandered back to her stool by then. so he pulled up the chair & rushed thru *the old gray mare.* as he was putting his tools away, a man came up & shoved more money in his hand & said "play sentimental journey." daddy explained again that all he knew was *the old gray mare* but the guy said "no, you play beautiful. beautiful."

so, daddy again sat on the chair, again played *the old gray mare,* then grabbed his took kit & split out the back door.

mom always turned me over to dad when i was upset. during my first marriage, i used to call them a lot: bo was always doing something that wiped me out. mom would talk to me awhile & pretty soon i'd be screaming & yelling & she'd say, "just a minute, dear" & yell for dad. he'd come on the phone & say "hullo, ma'am." & i'd feel better.

19.

when we moved to san lorenzo, kia used to pick up objects & hit me
with them. one time i was resting on the front room floor, my eyes
shut, a man next to me, & kia quietly stepped in & smashed me in the
face with a heavy metal toy. i thot for awhile i wouldnt be able to like
my own child.

she was mad about moving, i guess; & mad at me for leaving her
father (who she called "mommy" / they were closer than she & i
were. some men teased him about it but simon said he cared for her &
she loved him & damn rights she called him mommy.) if there was
more to it, i havent figured it out.

since she was just a year & a half, i figured maybe she could
unlearn violence; relearn affection. so everytime she hit me, i would
take her hands & say "no. do nice." & stroke her cheek. if she hit
someone else, same policy. hold her hands & say "do nice" touching
that person's cheek. it worked. it took a couple of months. (or maybe
it just took that long for her anger to wear off.)

20.

The Invalid

i asked for milk & lori brought me milk. i wanted graham crackers so
she fetched me graham crackers. (i am writing this in bed, at nite, &
angel just put the covers over his head so he could sleep.) reading
about zelda fitzgerald today, i sighed disconsolately "there is no one
who kisses my hand, smuggles me messages, sends candy & flowers."
angel puffed up: "there better not be!"
"why." i pouted.
"because i'm jealous."
"why."
"because i love you."
i snuggled into his lap. lori came in with flowers & strewed them on
the bed. wysteria.
later, angel returned, his hands cupped; "guess what i got for you."
"flowers."
"no."

"candy."

"no."

"*what* then."

"a magic egg." & he let me peek into his hands. "this egg is magic & if you eat it you will get better." he rolled it in his hands, then laid it on the bed. after he left, i looked at it. it was just an egg. but he had held it so lovingly, i decided to try eating it.

just before she went to bed, kia snuck in with a cup full of crushed hardboiled eggs & cracker crums. "i made this for you."

"o, thank you, bunnies! "

"it is this hi." & she moved her hand over the cup, curving as the pile of food curved over the top.

"yes, punkin."

"you eat it now & you feel better." she stepped carefully off the bed, trotted into the front room.

momma: book III

PLACENTA PREVIA: CAESARIAN

1.
the doctors standing over me &
we were all on friendly terms
but i could smell my burning flesh
& had felt the knife as well.
the anesthesiologist & i were so
witty, but all our jokes couldnt
make the spinal stop the pain,
so he closed the mask over my mouth.

& i woke in pain & there were yellow daisies
& more pain & you were ok but in some far room
in a cage of yr own. you had been taken so early,
& and you needed more womb, poor baby,
i want my baby & they kept me from you
"you've just had surgery!" & the needle
in my arm again. not until evening, when
another supervisor came on, she came to see
why i was so much trouble. "my baby, my baby" i sobbed
& the nurse said "see?" & the woman glared at her,
"of course shes upset! she wants to see her baby!"
& yr daddy put me in a chair & wheeled me to yr cage
& you were so tiny.
i thot you had a pretty tan
but they said it was jaundice.
yr tiny chest heaving & heaving & no one

told me i could touch you, no
one told me, not one doctor or nurse,
not yr father, & everything had to be so sterile
in yr cage so i twisted my hands & wept, rocking
to hold you my baby my baby & when they called
the doctor that night to come save you, they didnt
even wake me, they thot i was that weak after my
precious operation. o, child, the wonder is not
that it took us 16 months to love each other,
the wonder is that errors can be overcome.
that a baby torn from ones sleeping belly can be as loved
as a child held wet & red in exhausted arms.

& next day we covered our hands
with rubber with talcum on it
& reached into you, held yr tiny lonesome hands & prayed
"welcome, welcome baby. welcome little kia.
we cant wait to hold you. please honey, breathe well,
please breathe, please, o baby please."
& the doctors called it a miracle. & the next day
they let you out, & in to my arms o baby my breasts were
so swollen & when you turned yr tiny face to me, yr
little sleeping eyes, o child, but then they took you
right back & the 3rd day everything was windswept,
the whole day was a prayer,
yr tiny tired eyes still not open

& the 4th day i cried "let me out!"
& the doctor did & we rode home,
yr baby smell warm in my arms,
the children waiting & eager with presents,
a little frightened but
i was more frightened & wouldnt let anyone
touch you, no, she lived, wait til shes stronger
& i fell into bed, feeling guilty at turning the children away,

& so tired, o baby, neither of us was dead.
neither of us was dead.

& now. yr sister's father someplace away away & no
letters for 6 months, he didnt even tell her if his
second child came & gave her another sister.
she needs more of my love to make up for that aborted father,
but i love both of you (god forgive me!) i cannot
love her twice as much to make up for no father, i love
both of you.

& all those years nobody loved me
except her & i screamed at her & spanked her
& threw her on the bed & slammed the door when
i was angry & desperate for her fathers love,
& i cant undo all those times i frightened her
& she loved me, she still loves me, i cant undo needing &
being tortured with loneliness until i cried out at her,
who loved me even in my needy loneliness. & how
do mothers, unloved, love their children?
the wonder is that we do, we
do not leave the little girls
we cry out in our terror & we love our little girls
who *must* have a better life, they must
not wait eternally for men to love them & fill them up,
they must live & we do what we can & the wonder is
that mistakes are not permanent, that we can go insane
with pain & be locked away & come back loving
our babies, & they loving us & kissing us on the knee while
we stand bent over at the sink, weeping. the wonder is
that our children want us to be happy & they love us
& they know why we strike out & they love us, the ones
who were born red & wet, the ones who were lifted
delicately from our bellies, the ones who came to us
from some other bed, as desperate for love as we are, the wonder
is that theres enuf love to go around.
& we love. we love.

71

2.

i'm not sure its ended.
i lived the births, i wrote the poem,
but the children are calling me

& there is more
more to it than the spewing forth.
i made designs tonite & asked "now what?
do i put em in a drawer?"
if they were oil paintings, i could sell em
watch em hang in museums.
but theyre not. theyre just designs.
& the house so full! photos, drawings;
our every mood caught in stitches
or folded up in books.
those designs overcrowd the place & what excuse
do i have to give them away? christmas
is over. so here i sit with 2 kids whose lives grow
beyond me (some woman sneered at *me* in the parking lot
cause kia walked in front of *her car*!)
& designs, crowding the spaces.

a child with untameable curly blond hair. i call her kia,
pine nut person, & her eyes so open as she watches me try
to capture her,
as i try to
name her.

(the guilt again — write of her older sister — everyone loves
babies. what of the lonely 7 year old (7½, mommy!) watching tv
in the front room?) what of her?
what of yesterday when she chased the baby in my room & i screamed

OUT OUT GET OUT & she ran
right out but the baby stayed,
unafraid. what is it like to have
a child afraid of you. your own
child, your first child, the one
youre expected to be most nervous with, the one no one expects
you to be perfect with (except women in parking lots),
the one who must forgive you if either of you are to survive.
what, after the absolution. how
is it. do i never cause her to cry
again? do i learn, & never mistreat her?
even when for 6 days i have been trapped in the house listening
for coughs in the nite, my thighs heavy w disuse, & she runs in
when i'm trying to sneak some
privacy, then do i still not yell at her?
only quietly explain, "i cannot
stand it. i must have time, a
little time, a quiet space" & she
nods, & backs out, pulling the baby
w her. o is that better. you
woman sneering at me from yr car, you
white man telling me i must remove my baby
from the ballet, her delited dancing
disturbs the lead ass audience (you told me
i must go. but we stayed. we stayed.)

is that better. to state the pain
in quiet desperation & watch
her never be a child.
(childhood doesnt exist,
brenda reassured me) but when her
eyes look flat, when she knows so much,
did i educate her
too well, o, is it better, o could i
have done it any other way,
are there more than 2 answers,
when do i kno i did alright?

73

if i die before she does, then
did i do alright?

her every fear terrifies me.
"sometimes i think no one likes me"
she confessed. "sometimes i think yr all pretending"
& i wait for news from her father, i wait
for her to mention him, i wait
& wait "the function of a woman is to wait"
i read & leaned back in the rocking chair, relieved
that i finally knew what i was for, & why
w her in my belly i was a lady in waiting.
but i'm still waiting & she was born in 1964 —
maybe we are happy, & just dont know it.

the baby sucking her bottle & holding onto my knee
as i write this, my belly twisting w pain, if i go
to the other room she will follow me there, i am not yet allowed any

                perspective.

& how right is it to shut her out of the room so i can write about her?
how human, how loving, how can
i even try to
: name her.

maybe they could manage w/out me.
maybe i could steal
away a little time
in a different room
would they all still love me
when i came back?

3.
& now theyre away. & i miss them.
all the things i wanted to do while theyre with dad,
all those things are beige & grey; to see people who

74

love me less than the children do,
those adults who rarely call (i figured out today,
every woman friend who claims to love me but never
comes by, has children. do they think i would not
welcome their children? do they think they cannot move
w/o a babysitter? they get babysitters so they can go
to a movie. maybe if i charged them $2 theyd think
i was a movie.)

the house is silent. its nice sometimes to be quiet;
to have no interruptions. its nice to write something
longer than 6 lines. its nice to play a record & not
have to watch the record player. i wish i could enjoy it.

its nice to hold a warm little person,
to receive kisses & feel little arms around yr neck.

does it make any sense that raising children is a burden?
does it make any sense that we must always be in pain?

no. it doesnt.
it doesnt make any sense.
when indians saw white people spank their children,
they thot at first that whites hated their children,
then decided, since that was ridiculous, that it was a
religious rite. exorcism.
or something.

why must i be a watchdog for 24 hours?
& then, when quiet comes, why must i be lonely?

we live wrong.
our lives are wrong.
to trap us in houses with no help,
to be sole guardians for little people,
our lives are wrong.

& who will right them?
i am trying.
i cannot do it alone.
even for myself, i cannot
do it alone.

We at Times Change Press depend, in order to be a valid, responsive resource, on your critical and supportive *feedback*. Please, let us know what you think/feel about this book. We need to reverse the one-way communication of "mass" media by relating to individuals in as meaningful a way as possible. Please! Let us hear from you.

Books from Times Change Press

JANUARY THAW: People at Blue Mt. Ranch Write About Living Together in the Mountains. Writing about relationships, work, parents, children, healing and celebration, these rural communards describe feeling their way toward a life that makes sense and feels good, in which people are more in harmony with themselves, each other, the earth and the universe. *Illustrated; 160 pp; $3.25. Cloth, $8.50.*

THE EARLY HOMOSEXUAL RIGHTS MOVEMENT (1864-1935)—John Lauritsen and David Thorstad. The gay movement, like the women's movement, has an early history, which, beginning in 1864, advanced the cause of gay rights until the 1930s when Stalinist and Nazi repression obliterated virtually all traces of it. The authors uncover this history, highlighting interesting people and events. *Illustrated; 96 pp; $2.25. Cloth, $6.95.*

MOMMA: A Start on All the Untold Stories—Alta. This is Alta's intensely personal story of her life with her two young daughters, and her struggle to be a writer. She tells of her efforts toward self-fulfillment and her battle against feelings of guilt—a story many readers will recognize as their own. *Illustrated; 80 pp; $2.00. Cloth, $6.50.*

AMAZON EXPEDITION: A Lesbianfeminist Anthology—Edited by Phyllis Birkby, Bertha Harris, Jill Johnston, Esther Newton and Jane O'Wyatt. When lesbians within the gay liberation movement synthesized gay politics with feminism, they started a separate political/cultural development which thousands of women began to identify with. This is what this anthology is about. Culture, herstory, politics, celebration. Lesbianfeminism—one concept: the new womanity. *Illustrated; 96 pp; $2.25. Cloth, $6.50.*

LISTEN TO THE MOCKING BIRD: Satiric Songs To Tunes You Know—Tuli Kupferberg. Radical songs can't make the new world, but they can help. And they can help you endure this one. Especially if they're humorous. Over 50 songs to delight and thrill you and yes make you laugh. *Illustrated; 64 pp; $1.50.*

THIS WOMAN: Poetry of Love and Change—Barbara O'Mary. This journal tells of a year of intense change—involving Barbara's lovers male and female, her daughters, her job, her politics, her fears, her visions. Simple, intimate and honest poetry which we identify with immediately, as it clarifies our own experience. *Illustrated; 64 pp; $1.50.*

LESSONS FROM THE DAMNED: Class Struggle in the Black Community—By The Damned. This book describes the awareness of oppression as black people, as workers and poor people under capitalism, and as women and young people oppressed by men and the family. It may be the first time that poor and petit-bourgeois black people have told their own story. *Illustrated; 160 pp; $2.75. Cloth, $7.95.*

SOME PICTURES FROM MY LIFE: A Diary—Marcia Salo Rizzi. Marcia has selected entries from her diary and combined them with her emotionally powerful ink-brush drawings—one woman's experience reflecting pictures from the lives of all women. *Illustrated; 64 pp; $1.35.*

GREAT GAY IN THE MORNING!: One Group's Approach to Communal Living and Sexual Politics—The 25 to 6 Baking & Trucking Society. These are personal accounts of seven gay men and two lesbians writing about their experiences in over three years of communal living, gay consciousness-raising, and political involvement. *Illustrated; 96 pp; $2.25. Cloth, $4.95.*

BEGIN AT START: Some Thoughts on Personal Liberation and World Change—Su Negrin. A Times Change Press editor writes about her experiences in various liberation movements (mysticism, free school, commune, new left, feminist and gay) and talks about how they're all coming together in a new way—transforming individuals and approaching a utopia more awesome than we have ever dreamed of. *Illustrated; 176 pp; $2.75. Cloth, $6.95.*

YOUTH LIBERATION: News, Politics and Survival Information—Youth Liberation of Ann Arbor. The authors write about the oppression of being young in an adult chauvinist society—imprisonment in families and schools, economic dependence, denial of legal rights—and they describe the growing activity toward world-wide youth liberation. *Illustrated; 64 pp; $1.75.*

FREE OURSELVES: Forgotten Goals of the Revolution—Arthur Aron; Illustrations by Elaine N. Blesi. In our movement for social change, we have in many ways, lost touch with our humanistic values. Art believes that to realize our values we must *live* them—now—by changing ourselves and creating a giant personal/social/cultural alternative. *Illustrated; 64 pp; $1.35.*

WOODHULL AND CLAFLIN'S WEEKLY: The Lives and Writings of Victoria Woodhull and Tennessee Claflin—Arlene Kisner, Editor/Biographer. Throughout their notorious careers, Victoria and Tennie were involved in the radical developments of their time—socialism, mysticism, women's rights. These selections from their (in)famous newsmagazine (1870-1876) are interspersed with Arlene's detailed biographical sketches. *Illustrated; 64 pp; $1.35.*

UNBECOMING MEN: A Men's Consciousness-Raising Group Writes on Oppression and Themselves. This book reflects the struggles of a group of men who've come together because of their increasingly unavoidable awareness of sexism—how it operates against the people they most care for and ultimately, how it eats away at their own humanity. *Illustrated; 64 pp; $1.75.*

GENERATIONS OF DENIAL: 75 Short Biographies of Women in History—Kathryn Taylor. These women were whole people under the worst of circumstances, worse still for those who, in addition to being female, were gay. These biographies are a pioneering collection with which to supplement history books and women's pride. *Illustrated; 64 pp; $1.35.*

BURN THIS AND MEMORIZE YOURSELF: Poems for Women—Alta; Photographs by Ellen Shumsky. An unusual pamphlet of plain-talking poems, set against a background of photographs, showing women in many of the new ways they are beginning to be together—self-sufficient, intimate, loving, self-defined. *Illustrated; 16 pp; 50¢.*

FREE SPACE: A Perspective on the Small Group in Women's Liberation—Pamela Allen. *Free Space* is a good handbook for people wondering how to begin or restructure a consciousness-raising group. Developed by feminists, the small group is now being used by many people as a way of relating to different needs. *Illustrated; 64 pp; $1.75.*

ECOLOGY AND REVOLUTIONARY THOUGHT—Murray Bookchin. This book widens the scope of the ecological problem by asserting that people's domination over nature is rooted in our domination over each other. Murray takes into account the social/political crises that are inseparable from our environmental one. *Illustrated; 64 pp; $1.25.*

THE TRAFFIC IN WOMEN and Other Essays on Feminism—Emma Goldman; with a biography by Alix Kates Shulman. Emma Goldman was a dynamic anarchist and so her feminism differed markedly from her suffrage-oriented contemporaries. Today the split between liberal and radical approaches to women's liberation are still not resolved. So these essays have an uncanny relevancy to problems now being dealt with. *Illustrated; 64 pp; $1.35.*

WITH LOVE, SIRI AND EBBA—Siri Fraser and Ebba Pedersen. Siri and Ebba are two young women who decided to hitch-hike through northern Africa to Sudan and Ethiopia. These letters, drawings and photographs tell the story of their adventure and of their love for "the most fantastic free wild nomadic tribes" people, with whom they lived. *Illustrated; 128 pp; $3.25. Cloth, $8.50.*